D0561296

Bound-for-Career Guidebook

*A Student Guide to Career
Exploration, Decision Making, and the Job Search*

Second Edition

Frank Burtnett

ROWMAN & LITTLEFIELD
Lanham • Boulder • New York • London

Published by Rowman & Littlefield
A wholly owned subsidary of The Rowman & Littlefield Publishing Group, Inc.
4501 Forbes Boulevard, Suite 200, Lanham, Maryland 20706
www.rowman.com

6 Tinworth Street, London SE11 5AL, United Kingdom

British Library Cataloguing in Publication Information Available

Library of Congress Cataloging-in-Publication Data

Library of Congress Control Number: 2020942349
ISBN 978-1-4758-4838-0 (cloth)
ISBN 978-1-4758-4840-3 (electronic)

Dedicated to my adventurous life partner, Susan; my children, Kevin and Kimberly; and their partners, Brenda and Robert.

Each is a person of unique intelligence, special talent, and extraordinary personality. Each has found success and satisfaction in their respective careers and lives. Individually and collectively, they have made my life more complete with their presence in it.

~

Contents

List of Student Exercises

~

Career Facts and Myths

Facts

- Many people will engage in careers that didn't exist when they started school.
- Success in certain occupations can best be achieved by those possessing specific characteristics and traits.
- Statistics are important in examining the present and future of any career.
- More than four thousand US institutions offer degree-granting postsecondary education opportunities in the United States.
- The more you learn, the more you earn.
- Networking is a valuable tool for one to use throughout the career development process.
- Experience plays a meaningful role in a worker's career advancement.

Myths

- There is one perfect career for each individual.
- Career development resembles a ladder that one climbs from entry to retirement.
- The United States is the land of opportunity, and there are always occupations that are open for people who wish to work.

- Career opportunities are restricted to educational and training achievements and levels.
- Elite colleges produce the most successful leaders in the United States.
- Having no experience is detrimental to entry-level job seekers.
- Salary is the number-one contributor to worker satisfaction.

~

Introduction

High on the list of life decisions that are made by adolescents and young adults will be the ones that determine what they will study and how they will prepare for the major portion of their life called their career. Although the US workplace affords many and varied career options, the process of determining what to do with one's life remains a significant challenge. Each decision must be followed by purposeful action to result in goal achievement. Eventually the totality of those decisions and actions can result in career success and attainment.

The *Bound-for-Career Guidebook* views career identification, selection, entry, and progression as part of a larger developmental process—the career development process. I believe so strongly in this concept that chapter 2 focuses on just how individuals progress developmentally—from childhood to the senior years—through this process.

Our careers and lives are intertwined in ways more complex than one will realize until later in life. Many say the work we do defines us. Others point to the realization of ambition and achievement of goals as two of the most important things we do in our lives. Similarly, not being where we want to be in our career can lead to anxiety and frustration.

Clearly, women and men who have entered the US workplace in the current millennium are placing a higher premium on a life-work balance. Further, career and job satisfaction is no longer strictly associated with compensation and benefits. The contemporary worker seeks a new form of engagement that is noticeably different from that of just a few years ago.

This book addresses the incredible importance that change plays in education and career. Students across the United States will work one day in careers that didn't exist the day they started school. Current workers who thought their "school days" were over when they earned their diploma, certificate, or degree are learning the true meaning of "lifelong" learning. What we need to know and the skills required for performing our work roles are affected dramatically by change, and all workforce members must possess the ability to learn and adapt.

Readers are encouraged to engage in experiences that will bring about a sense of understanding as to who they are (i.e., self-awareness) and how they can use that knowledge to look ahead at the paths (i.e., educational and career awareness) that will result in career success and satisfaction. Don't expect the career journey to be easy or offer any guarantees. It is also about controlling what is controllable, making sound decisions, and acting in a manner that achieves the desired results. Empowered students and workers are better able to guide themselves through their personal career journey. The command of the information in the *Bound-for-Career Guidebook* will give readers that power!

~

CHAPTER ONE

Career Success

Actions that Lead to Achievement and Satisfaction

The best way to predict the future is to create it.

—Peter Drucker, writer,
consultant, and self-described "social ecologist"

This is a book about the future—your future. It is about the work that you will do one day and how your work will affect your life and living. It is about the options you will have before you and what you must do to make quality decisions that allow you to achieve your full potential.

The average American spends approximately 11,500 days in the workplace over a typical span of more than forty years. That's a lot of time. Your work is going to influence your ability to do a lot of the things that you want to do. It will send you down certain paths of preparation and then even more paths as you attempt to find the best place to practice the profession or craft you have mastered. Finally, it will guide you through a self-determined web of opportunities that will promote career mobility, growth, and achievement—and hopefully a measure of career success as you move throughout your life span.

Ten Elements that Shape and Influence Careers

There are a number of factors that will play a significant role in your personal career development. The more you know, understand, and can control these factors, the better you will manage what you do and what happens to you along the way. As you move through your life's career transitions, allow these ten thoughts to guide your journey:

1. Know that you have a unique set of individual characteristics. To plan realistically, you must appraise yourself honestly and fairly. There is only one you.
2. Recognize that routes to careers and occupations vary, and different people may use a different map to get to the same place.
3. Seek to learn as much about yourself, your environment, and the world of work as you can. Solicit the views of others about you and the traits and characteristics that best describe you. The appropriate use of assessment tools and techniques will add to this understanding.
4. Make the most of every educational experience. Knowledge might just become the most powerful influence you will have in your life.
5. Become a student of the US workplace and the skills needed to navigate it. Get "up close and personal" in your study of educational and career opportunities.
6. Seek the help of counselors, educators, family, and friends who are positioned to help you in achieving your full educational and career potential.
7. Devote the time and energy necessary to study who you are, where you are, where you want to go, and the various paths that may be followed to get there.
8. Recognize the importance of "change" in yourself and in the world that surrounds you. Inability to accept and manage change could produce devastating results. Flexibility and adaptability promote opportunity.
9. Recognize the value of service learning and volunteerism in exploring work roles and environments, and gain as much exposure of this nature as you can.
10. Practice behaviors that promote personal wellness and health.

Several Definitions to Consider
Understanding the meaning of terms such as *career, occupation, vocation,* and *job* may be useful at this juncture. Throughout our growing years, many hold jobs that result in getting paid for the work they perform. Often our first jobs are babysitting, lawn mowing, and other similar tasks. Sometimes they are more defined like restaurant server, camp counselor, or lifeguard. Many jobs are short term or temporary and provide a source of income as we "bridge" from one place in our life to another.

The term *job* is one that will be used throughout the career development process. Often it is more convenient to refer to *job search*, *job posting*, and *job interview*. Remember, however, that the jobs and occupations that you experience will lead to a larger aspect of your life—your career.

An *occupation* or *vocation* is a more precise work role. It is defined as a formally classified work activity in which a person fills or performs a role such as teacher, systems analyst, nurse, or pilot. Occupations typically require preparation for, and performance of, a set of responsibilities established by an employer. The term *vocation* has been used historically to identify workplace skills (e.g., auto mechanics, culinary arts, graphic design, etc.) that are taught in a vocational education, apprenticeship, or training setting.

Career, as it will be referenced in this book, is defined as the totality of the experiences held by a person over her or his life span. That totality will include learning psychological, sociological, and related elements as they influence entry and progression through the individual's "life work." Often the terms *career* and *occupation* will be used interchangeably.

The Ultimate Goal: Career Success
Career success need not be elusive. It is about being in control and using your talents and skills in the workplace to achieve the goals that you have set for yourself. Success will mean different things to different people. For most, it will involve how well they prepare for, enter, and progress through their chosen career. For others, like the entrepreneur, it will be measured in how well the business succeeds and turns an expected profit. Many aspects of success will be defined by you—using your benchmarks. Once people find themselves in their chosen career, it is not unusual for them to set longer term (e.g., "Where do I want to be in five years . . . ten years . . .") objectives.

That is not to say that others and other factors will not be influential. Some of these factors are controllable; others are less so. Opportunities to grow, change, and practice mobility, for example, are often affected by the economy. Competition in the workplace will vary dramatically from one situation to another. Many workplace situations are more volatile than others. There are right and wrong times to venture into the entrepreneurial world where goods and services are being offered via a new business enterprise.

People's success in a chosen career is going to depend highly on their ability to address and handle change. The world in which we work is constantly changing. The tools and information we use are improving and being made more accessible. The organizational structures and protocols of the workplace are being updated and enhanced. The only predictable aspect of change is that it will never cease. Your adaptability—sometimes to the unknown and the difficult to imagine—may be required if you are to be truly successful.

Ultimately, the most important measure of your career success is you. Do you enjoy what you are doing? Have you achieved what you wanted to achieve? Are you growing and developing in your work? At some distant point in your future, positive responses to most or all of these questions will mean you were successful.

Career Myth: There Is One Perfect Career for Each Individual

Perfection in career attainment is a wonderful goal, but most must settle for something short of that ideal. One of the great things about career exploration is the number of opportunities and options that will open for you as you travel the various educational and career paths before you. Recognize also how you and your preferences are going to change as you gain knowledge, skills, and experiences. Those factors alone will make perfection, at best, a moving target.

Finally, forget the "one" notion. There are lots of perfect careers waiting for you in the world of work.

Frequently Asked Questions

Question: What role will luck play in what career I enter some day?

Answer: Luck is defined as a chance happening—good or bad. On the positive side, you may have heard someone say they were at the "right place at the right time," and something good happened as a result. By exposing themselves to as many career possibilities as they can during the exploration process, career seekers increase the chances of learning about work opportunities. Knowledge breeds opportunity and the chance for positive results. Learn as much as you can and make quality decisions and you will maximize the personal control you have over your career destiny and minimize how much of your future is left to luck and chance.

Question: How often do Americans change occupational positions?

Answer: The US Department of Labor's Bureau of Labor Statistics does not keep numbers about "career changers" because this work characteristic is almost impossible to monitor. Some people change careers deliberately as they move through life, obtain new experiences, and point themselves toward where they want to be. For them, it is a matter of progression through a series of career experiences, each building on the last.

Others do so involuntarily. Take, for example, the elementary school teacher who becomes unemployed because of "downsizing" in a school district and finds employment with a lawn service for a period of one year before finding another teaching position. Did the teacher truly change jobs or simply perform another occupation while seeking another teaching position? Another change that is difficult to appraise is when a Web designer leaves a job to create a start-up Web design firm. Is this a career change or a natural progression within one's career? For these and other reasons, you will not find career change statistics from the US Department of Labor.

~

CHAPTER TWO

Understanding the Career Development Process

By failing to prepare, you are preparing to fail.

—Benjamin Franklin, statesman, printer, writer, and inventor

The career development process represents a series of life stages and events, during which a person explores, selects, prepares for, enters, and progresses through an occupation or career. It starts early and continues across the life span. Everyone experiences this process, and it helps if you know what is happening and how you can influence it.

The more you recognize the order of these events and the tasks that must be performed, the greater the likelihood that more positive outcomes will occur. Everyone would like to enter a career that brings satisfaction and comfort, one that allows them to realize their full human potential and will permit them to enjoy a work style and lifestyle that is to their liking. Choice points in the career development process are more obvious and distinguishable. They are the intersections in the career development process when a person must stop or slow down and make a decision—a time at a crossroads or fork in the road and decide among the options that lie ahead.

Understanding the entire process and the various stages within the career development process will allow you to capitalize on what is happening when it is happening. Knowing gives you a power that can become influential in your selections of, and transition into, a career. The stages of the career development process are provided in figure 2.1.

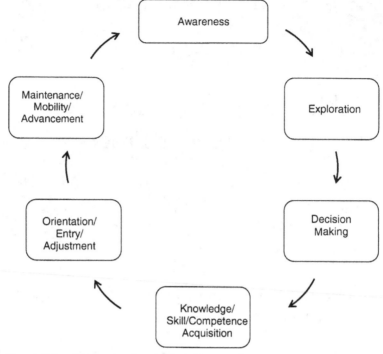

Figure 2.1. Career development process

Awareness

This initial stage represents the time when individuals, usually during their youth, begin to get a "sense of self" through a thorough examination of their aptitudes, achievements, interests, personality traits, lifestyle preferences, and values. It is a process that is repeated many times with each new experience contributing their self-awareness.

During awareness, the individual is first able to answer, "Who am I?" in a realistic fashion and, for the first time, relates that understanding of self to the world around them. As individuals move through adolescence and young adulthood, they continue in this self-learning as new aspects of personal awareness come into view, and they are able to address each from a more mature perspective.

Exploration

During this stage people begin to create questions and search for answers that broaden their career or work understanding. It is also a time when individuals relate what they have learned about themselves to their investigation of the educational and occupational choices they are considering. Information, both human and media (i.e., print, computer, etc.), plays a key role in addressing exploration questions and care should be taken to ensure that the information is accurate and current.

Informational experiences (i.e., career shadowing, volunteerism, part-time employment) can be valuable contributors during the exploration stage. This time of exploration continues throughout the youth and young adult years. It is also a time when individuals set goals and recognize they are evolving, maturing individuals; this period of discovery continues for some time.

Decision Making

Rather than a stage of the career development process, decision making represents an event or multiple events that occur over time—situations in which individuals must choose from among options they have identified. The decisions people make may be time oriented, like determining what subjects to study in school or which summer or part-time job to seek.

Others, like selecting a college major or determining whether to engage in volunteerism or service learning, may be more influential in the larger scheme of one's life or career. Decisions beget decisions, and not knowing that they exist is tantamount to giving up personal control of the career development process. Not knowing a decision lies before you increases the chances that the decision will be made for you and not by you.

Knowledge/Skill Acquisition and Competence Attainment

Following each education and career decision, individuals must take deliberate steps to acquire occupational knowledge, and a skill set to make them a marketable candidate for employment. Competence is also acquired by engagement in the tasks associated with the occupational role and the experience that is gained from that early exposure. Any form of hands-on experience (i.e., work study, internship, part-time employment, or volunteer work) will add to that competence level and become a valuable résumé enhancer.

Knowledge + Skill + Experience = Competence

Figure 2.2. Competence Attainment

The knowledge and skill set acquired across the schooling experiences (K–12, career/technical studies, and all forms of postsecondary education), as well as the on-the job and continuing education experiences over a career, result in basic career knowledge and skills to keep current with respect to emerging techniques, trends, and tools.

Orientation, Entry, and Adjustment

This stage represents a "bridging" time, a period of transition when individuals relate where they are to where they want to be. In many settings, this period is referred to as onboarding. It is a time when people seek to apply their marketable knowledge or skills in the workplace. It can also be a time of renewed awareness of their abilities, interests, and personal characteristics, but now this knowledge is being applied to the environments or settings (e.g., location, firm size, etc.) where they would like to work. It is when job finding and acquisition strategies (e.g., résumé creation, acquiring interview skills, etc.) must be learned and executed.

Many prospective job changers are people not dissatisfied with their career but rather individuals who are uncomfortable in the particular environment where they are working. This discomfort can be with the philosophy or an employer's point of view, potential for growth, salary, workplace compatibility, or related issues. A part of adjusting to a career is adjusting to the culture of the workplace, and often individuals must try several employment settings before they find a good fit.

Growth, Mobility, and Maintenance

The longer people work in their chosen career and achieve a measure of success, the more likely it will be that they will receive added responsibilities and rewards (e.g., promotions, salary adjustments, etc.). During this part of the career development process, a significant number of individuals learn that they have outgrown their particular circumstance and will elect to look elsewhere to realize their full career potential.

Some individuals simply outgrow their initial or entry career situation and seek to exit one position or work setting and reenter another that affords them new opportunities and greater challenges. Any new knowledge or skill set acquisition, coupled with experience in job performance, will add to any growth and mobility opportunities.

During the growth, mobility, and maintenance stage, some individuals may also have to face the difficult situations of termination or job loss as a result of downsizing, inadequate job performance, inadequate preparation, or some other concern. These situations require a revisiting of the previous stages of the career development process to refresh, refocus, and possibly move forward in a different direction. Unlike the orientation, entry, and adjustment stage, these situations can result in personal discomfort and stress for individuals who have found themselves suddenly unemployed or drastically underemployed for the first time. They are delicate life circumstances and need to be treated as such.

Winding Down, Adjustment, and Exit

This is the time in people's life when they elect to ease up on the accelerator and even apply the brakes as it relates to their career. This stage should never be construed as final or the end of anything. Deceleration is simply the act of slowing down, making changes in time devoted to work, reducing the tasks that are performed, and adjusting to a revised work style (i.e., three-day work week, telecommuting, etc.). It also will afford them greater time for family, friends, and leisure pursuits.

Increased life expectancy and other factors (e.g., economic, social, etc.) have kept older workers in the workforce. In many instances this has been voluntary because individuals prefer a life of activity and challenges to the more reticent and detached lifestyle that retirement and retreat from the workplace may present. They do not want to stop working, and many others have opted for flexible schedules that allow them to mix continued work with opportunities for enhanced leisure pursuits. In some instances, remaining employed at a later age is not voluntary but is tied directly to the need to keep a steady source of income to ensure economic stability.

Career Development Is a Cyclical Process

The reader must understand that the process just described is cyclical and not linear. Many times an explorer will make decisions and act on them, only to return to exploration again at some point in the future. As people mature, move from one environment to another, or learn more things about themselves, they may wish to revisit previous stages in the process. The dynamics of human growth and development demand that the career development process be dynamic as well.

Eventually all of the exploring, deciding, and learning places the individual in a position to enter and process through an occupation or career field. When a series of work experiences are pieced together over time, a career is created—a body of work that reflects much more than the day-to-day experiences. Our work often becomes more—a reflection of our personality and our ability to face challenges and move through them to display our worth and productivity.

Career Myth: Career Development Resembles a Ladder that One Climbs from Entry to Retirement

If you think of career development as merely moving up the rungs of a ladder, this linear view is too narrow and restrictive. From early in our lives, we hear about "climbing the ladder" to achieve success. Rather than thinking of career development as a ladder comprised of vertical moves, consider it more like a lattice, a structure where career adjustments are both vertical (north and south) and horizontal (east and west). In reality, members of the workforce move in multidirectional ways, gaining experience and learning to multitask. It is these kinds of experiences in the contemporary workplace that make a person a valued contributor and one most likely to be considered when promotion and advancement opportunities arise.

Frequently Asked Questions

    Question: At what point in my life should I know what career I wish to enter?

    Answer: It varies from person to person. Some will say that their interest in a career could be traced all the way back to their childhood. Others will say they started connecting with the world of work as they studied different subjects in school. Still others point to experiences observing, volunteering, or actually working as the indicator that sent them down a particular career path. Don't panic if you are not clear about what you want to do for your life's work. It happens at different times for different people.

    Question: With life expectancy increasing in recent times, how long can I expect to work in my lifetime?

    Answer: According to the Social Security Administration, life expectancy at birth in 1930 was only 58 for men and 62 for women. The Centers for Disease Control and Prevention figures for 2017 projected women can expect to live to 81.1 years and men 76.1. Living longer has resulted in a greater percentage of persons older than age of 65 in the workforce, a statistic influenced by better health and living circumstances. Clearly, many older people are opting for situations that keep their career active but often in accordance with a reduced or flexible work schedule. Work is a healthy behavior, and many do not wish to give it up. For some, continued work is a way of ensuring greater economic stability for the time when retirement becomes a reality.

Question: Wouldn't your career become incredibly boring if you did the same thing every day for the rest of your life?

Answer: Whether your work is boring has a lot to do with your personality. Repetitious routine on an automotive assembly line could be viewed by some as something they would hate doing and do everything to avoid. Others would view the same role as contributing their piece to the larger product—the car that rolls off the assembly line. Contrasting points of view like this stress why it is important for people to get an accurate grasp of their personal traits, likes, dislikes, and other characteristics so the "who you are" can be considered as you move into and through your life's work. Even individuals who perform work roles that are uniform or repetitive find diverse ways of approaching these tasks and their daily routine.

~

CHAPTER THREE

The Importance of Career Exploration, Decision Making, and Goal Setting

Without goals, and plans to reach them, you are like a ship without a destination.

—Fitzhugh Dodson, psychologist

"What do you want to be when you grow up?" is a question that you may be asked at multiple times in your youth. Caring and concerned parents, family members, and friends are usually the ones doing the asking, but eventually you may also find it posed to you by an interested teacher or counselor. Those ten words, however, may constitute the most challenging question—and most difficult to answer—you will ever be asked. Why?

Most people, especially during their youth and young adult years, don't know enough about themselves or the prospects for the future to accurately and responsibly answer this question. Responding also requires the elimination of so many options while zeroing in on one, two, or maybe three careers in a world that includes tens of thousands of opportunities. While narrowing options and selecting among choices will eventually happen, it shouldn't be forced on any individual who is not ready.

Another thing that makes answering this question a challenge is the change that is rampant in the workplace and the roles that people play there. It is reasonable to expect that many reading this book will enter occupations and careers that do not exist at this moment. Some futurists believe that one in six kindergarten students today will eventually pursue careers that didn't exist the day they started school. The career you enter and spend the majority of your working life in may not exist today.

Some occupations have been around seemingly forever, while others are disappearing as technology, science, and related innovations discover new ways of doing things. But those same factors that have led to job obsolescence have also altered how many careers are performed in the contemporary workplace. Few careers of yesterday are performed exactly the same way today.

No one intends harm in asking you about your future, and if anything, they may highlight for you the important role that exploration must play before you can be an effective decision maker. Then, and only then, are you equipped to answer the "What do you want to be when you grow up" question.

Making decisions too early requires that you choose among options before you have learned what you need to know about yourself and the world of work in general. As an adolescent or young adult, you're still in the process of growing, maturing, and evolving into the person you will one day be. That's the individual who is going to get an education, find a job, and build a career over time.

The awareness and exploration period can actually be quite enjoyable. It is a natural time to "fantasize" about the future. Locking into career choices this early, however, may not be the wisest action. True self-understanding is just beginning, and your knowledge of the world of work is ever expanding, albeit limited. Consider, as well, that unknown element called "change" and how it might influence what you know and what you wish to do.

It is during the exploration stage that you may set tentative goals, recognizing that you too are evolving and maturing. Your maturation is a journey that opens doors and windows of opportunity and promise. Each of the environments you experience in this journey—home, school, and work—becomes a learning place. To make major educational and career decisions too early is to cut short or eliminate a lot of this learning.

Exploration is a time when you look into the worlds of education and work as if you were looking into a mirror. Do you see yourself there? Is that what you want to study? Are the career environments compatible with what you know about yourself and where you see yourself working one day? Quality career decision making and goal setting happens best when it has been preceded by your completion of a number of tasks. These include:

1. Gaining a sense of self-awareness by examining your aptitudes, interests, achievements, values, and preferences. This self-understanding will enhance your ability to make the decisions that lie before you in the career development process.
2. Acquiring a basic knowledge of the work world and the paths to different careers within. One thing you will learn is that some routes to

some occupations and careers are fixed and regimented. Others offer multiple avenues for the individual to pursue. Your objective is to create or find the best map from where you are to where you want to be.

3. Experiencing firsthand as many different work roles and career settings as you can. Through part-time work, summer jobs, volunteering, and other forms of service learning, you will enjoy experiential learning that can only be acquired through "trying something on to see how it fits."

A Formula for Making Effective Decisions
Benjamin Franklin is most remembered in history as a founding father, diplomat, and inventor, but he is also credited with creating a time tested decision-making model. It occurred when he was asked by a friend for advice on making a personal decision. In his response, Franklin suggested his friend divide the decision-making task into a series of steps, including:

1. Frame the decision as a yes-or-no proposition.
2. List the pros and cons or consequences of the various options.
3. Assess their importance.
4. Assess the probability of each option being achieved.
5. Weigh and prioritize options accordingly.
6. Strike out any offsetting pros and cons.
7. Review, reflect, and then decide.
8. Evaluate the decision.

Many decisions that we make are signaled well ahead of their occurrence. These are the more friendly decisions because they permit us to structure the response in the manner suggested by Franklin. Others are more spontaneous and require more immediate action. The worst scenario is not knowing there is a decision before you or failing to see it on the horizon and not allowing sufficient time to identify and consider the options. Knowing when you have to decide is another important element in the equation.

Our failure to recognize or pay appropriate attention to the educational and career decisions that lie before us can result in two outcomes, both negative. One result is the loss of personal power because others may slip into the decision-maker role and make them for us. The second is a less-than-quality decision resulting from the failure to apply a decision-making model.

The decisions that you will make about your future will have both an immediate and a long-term effect. They also have a certain element of irreversibility about them. As people implement a decision, they make a number of investments:

- Time—Each poor decision is a time "bandit." Pursuit of an incorrect or poor choice robs the decision maker of time, which is an investment that can't be recouped.
- Expense—There is often a financial cost associated with poor decision making. If you pay tuition, room and board, and related expenses to engage in an educational experience or training that was not the best one for you, those expenditures can be an unrecoverable investment.
- Ego—People want to do the right thing, and they want their decisions to be successful once made. When you throw yourself into the awareness and exploration process and then make decisions about the future, you want them to be the right ones. It's natural for there to be a certain "ego" investment in being right. When that decision goes awry or fails to produce desirable or successful results, some will look at that failure as an attack on their psyche.

I want to make a confession here. The last step (number 8) in the decision-making model presented previously was not advanced by Benjamin Franklin. It is mine. Decision making is such a critical part of the career development process that each significant decision made requires monitoring and evaluation as a part of follow-up. When the expected outcome does not occur or is not at the level expected, decisions need to be reconsidered, and if necessary, alternative actions put into place. This evaluation will bring the appropriate "return on investment" for every decision made.

Good decision makers learn from their errors, get up and "dust off," and then move forward with an alternative decision. It is better to reverse a bad decision than to spend a lifetime "sentenced" to a career or occupation that is not the right one.

Setting Goals and Acting to Achieve Them

As you move through the developmental process achieving a sense of self and gaining an understanding of the varied educational and career options that lie before you, a natural next step is to use this information to point yourself toward the future, converting self-knowledge and awareness of opportunities into ambitions and goals. Goals can be both short term (immediate) and long term (futuristic). As you progress through the career development process, short-term goals (such as getting a particular summer job or winning a scholarship competition) are likely to be set, each becoming a focal point for the immediate future. Over time, these goal experiences and achievements will form a pattern, and the goals will become larger and have a greater impact on your future career direction.

A short-term goal for a student interested in becoming an environmental engineer would be to enroll in and achieve academic success in the most relevant and challenging mathematics and sciences courses available in high school and college. Another short-term goal might be to expose oneself to work, internship, and volunteer experiences that bring the individual close to the world of environmental engineering. Each represents a step along the way toward the eventual long-term target of becoming an environmental engineer.

Career achievement goals tend to be long term with objectives set further out in the future. Some long-term goals may also have intermediate indicators on course toward their achievement. Take, for example, the long-distance runner who wants to eventually run a marathon (26 miles, 385 yards). The runner may set 10, 15, and 20 miles as interval goals leading up to the full marathon. Few novice runners are capable of running the full distance the first time out.

Career goals allow you to plan an implementation strategy and, like the marathon runner, work toward intermediate achievements. Intermediate goals (e.g., completing high school, earning a college degree, obtaining an internship, etc.) keep you pointed and progressing toward your long-range goal. It is fine to set the bar high when setting goals, but your ambition should be realistic and achievable or it may be unattainable.

Career Fact: Many People Will Engage in Careers that Didn't Exist When They Started School

Proof of the incredible changes that are going on in the world of work is the fact that occupations such as data miner, forensic counselor, experimental petrologist, and wind farmer have come into the workplace in just the last few years. No wonder then that your parents—also possibly older siblings or you—have never heard of them. These occupations reflect the strong influence that discovery, technology, and innovation have on the work that people do in the United States and throughout the global community.

By the way, a data miner uses numbers and statistics to forecast events, explain business procedures, and generate predictive models. A forensic counselor uses knowledge of mental health law, with a specific focus on adult and juvenile justice, to assist legal and criminal justice systems in determining the proper resolution of cases and the most effective treatment for offenders. An experimental petrologist is one who studies rocks from other planets to learn about their formation and evolution, thus providing information as to whether there is life on other planets. Finally, wind farmers are likely to play a significant role in the energy we will use in the future; they monitor land areas, air speeds, turbine sizes, and the pitch of the windmill blades to generate the maximum amount of electric energy the wind farms of the future can generate.

Frequently Asked Questions

Question: How do you prepare for a career that doesn't exist yet?

Answer: The best way to prepare for the future is to pursue interests that make the most of your aptitudes, abilities, and achievements, eventually selecting classes and courses in high school or college that prepare you for the career of your choice. You must be an "explorer" and maybe even a "risk taker," seizing every opportunity to change direction should a new career emerge while you are studying or working.

Question: Right now, a number of different things appeal to me as career options. How do I narrow the list?

Answer: First, and very importantly, don't rush anything. Keep alive all of the genuine interests that you have long enough to give each a full review. Individuals with multiple career interests are likely candidates for the "try work on and see how it fits" exercise.

Arrange some "shadowing" experiences that will allow you to see the various careers and the individuals performing them. Look for volunteer, part-time work, and internship opportunities that will get you on the inside where you can test your interest and see if it is genuine. Don't allow one or two exposures to affect you positively or negatively but rather look to a mosaic of your experiences and what they tell you about the career. The information gained from these hands-on experiences will help you narrow your career selection list.

Question: How does one separate fantasy from reality when looking at the world of work?

Answer: Fantasy plays a legitimate role in our future gazing and enlivens how people look at their career prospects. What young athlete hasn't looked at his or her favorite soccer or basketball player performing on television and experienced the "what if" phenomenon? That's fantasy at work.

The reality is that upward of the 350,000 student athletes at National Collegiate Athletic Association (NCAA) institutions only a few hundred in any given year will move on to careers as professional athletes. The vast majority will be engineers, educators, business officials, and other members of the workforce. Reality sets in as individuals mature and gain an understanding of how their skills and talents compare to those qualities with the requirements of the various career fields.

Student Exercise 3.1

My Dream Career: A Look into the Crystal Ball

In the best of scenarios, what do you see as the perfect career for yourself? List it below. If multiple careers are currently on your radar screen, list them all.

_____

_____

What is it about the career or careers that you have listed above that is most appealing to you?

_____

_____

Do you believe your ideal career to be a realistic choice?
            Yes   No   Don't know yet

Do you see any challenges or problems in your eventual pursuit of your perfect career?
            Yes   No   Don't know yet

If yes, what are those challenges or problems?

_____

_____

What short-term career or educational goals should you set now to point you toward the achievement of your dream career?

_____

_____

CHAPTER FOUR

~

Learning about Yourself

Implications for Your Future Career

The future ain't what it used to be.

—Yogi Berra, New York Yankees Hall of Fame catcher

The career that you eventually enter and progress through is going to have a strong impact on your life. Work is a form of self-expression, an outlet for each individual to display his or her knowledge, talent, and skill. The more you like what you do and the greater the "fit" between you and your work, the greater the chance that you will achieve career satisfaction and success. This chapter addresses the ingredients that go into creating that fit.

Imagine, for a moment, you are in a classroom at school surrounded by fellow students who are like you in many ways. But, in actuality, how much are you really alike? You are in the same grade, the same age, live in the same community, and represent possibly some other elements of sameness. A number of your fellow students are accomplished athletes and play on the school teams. You participate in intramural sports. Two of your fellow students write for the school paper, and several participate in drama activities and participate in chorus. Several are active in doing volunteer service, and a number hold part-time jobs working after school and during the summer. You aren't into any of those things.

You have some classmates who thrive on academic and athletic competition and others who see such competition as their nemesis and do everything to avoid it. You get above-average grades and usually find yourself on the honor roll. A couple of students are really into art and writing, while you don't seem to have a creative bone in your body. Some students are "joiners" and thrive on interaction with others, but you find comfort and solace in doing things on your own.

These are just a few of the things that begin to explain how we are different—what counselors and educators refer to as *individual differences*. Differences don't have to take on a positive or negative connotation; they just help explain how you are different from your peers. The behavioral and emotional traits that define you represent your personality, a set of characteristics that distinguish you from others. These traits may eventually tell you things that can affect your immediate and future career decisions.

But first, you have to know the ways in which people differ. There are a number of individual elements—things that distinguish you from others—that will eventually complete the puzzle known as you. They include abilities, aptitudes, achievements, interests, personality traits, values, and lifestyle preferences. Alone, each is a piece of you. Collectively, they represent the person you are at this given moment. Over time, they can have a significant influence on your career development.

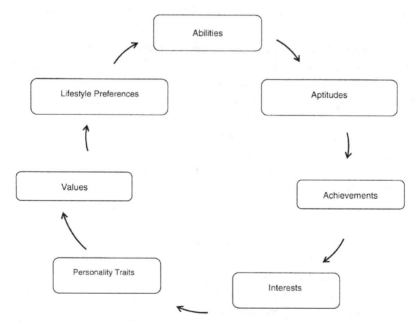

Figure 4.1.   Factors influencing personal awareness

Abilities
Abilities are the talents and capabilities that you display. They may have come to the surface in your schoolwork (e.g., doing research for a paper,

public speaking, etc.) or in your daily life (e.g., ability to lead or organize an event, manage money, etc.). Abilities emerge as you have new and different life experiences and as you grow and mature. They also send signals to us about the activities at which we excel and are indicators of skill areas that may have connections to future careers.

Aptitudes
Aptitudes represent your capacity for learning, your natural ability to do something. You have probably heard someone characterized in one of the following ways: "She's a natural athlete" or "He's a born debater." Each characterization is likely a description of that individual's aptitude for something. Aptitudes can range from academic things like writing or mathematics to other talents like acting, playing a musical instrument, or displaying a particular form of athletic potential.

Achievements
Achievements are the measured accomplishments in your life, those things that you have done well and for which you received recognition. They include things like earning good grades, setting a school record for career rebounds on the basketball team, or collecting the most food for the homeless at Thanksgiving. Often your achievements are formally recognized, like being named to the school honor roll or earning a holiday bonus at your part-time job.

Interests
Interests are the things you like to do, spend time doing, and arouse your curiosity. Sometimes they are spin-offs of your aptitudes, like an interest in writing or playing a guitar. Other times, they are simply things you enjoy and do just for fun—like collecting sports cards, cooking, or taking photographs. Often our interests generate emotions or feelings that cannot be experienced elsewhere. Runners, for example, often report they like the "zone" they get into in the midst of their daily run. Because interests are voluntarily engaged in by the individual, any pressure to achieve satisfaction in the pursuit of one's interests comes from within. When an interest diminishes or passes, one simply moves on to other interests and pursuits.

Personality Traits
Personality traits are the collection of characteristics that make you different from other people. Some of these traits are behavioral, and others are emotional and social. Words like *outgoing, quiet, attentive, inquisitive,* and

studious come to mind when thinking about personality traits. One should practice caution, however, and not fall into the trap of creating personality stereotypes of careers and people who perform them. In his book, *The Right Stuff*, Thomas Wolfe writes about the original astronaut corps of the National Aeronautics and Space Administration (NASA). Accomplished and successful in different ways, the men chosen for the early US space program possessed an array of personality traits that defied stereotyping.

Personality traits can also be misinterpreted and linked incorrectly to characteristics needed by various members of the workforce. There is a distinct line between someone who is assertive and someone who is aggressive. To some, being assertive is a positive trait, whereas being aggressive can have a negative connotation. People who are going to be engaged in sales and marketing careers will most likely benefit from an assertive personality. Others with the identical trait may find it an obstacle to their career success.

Values

Values are the aspects of your life that matter to you, those you hold in esteem, and the principles you espouse, stand behind, and would fight to maintain. A commitment to family, loyalty to your school or team, and your religious and spiritual beliefs are excellent examples. Along with all of the other characteristics discussed here, values help shape one's psyche and will influence the kind of work you opt to perform and the settings in which you choose to work. A person who values closeness, teamwork, and regular interaction with colleagues may elect to perform his or her accountant role in a smaller accounting firm or department as opposed to a large government agency or a mega firm.

Lifestyle Preferences

Lifestyle preferences are similar to values but may be just a bit more practical. They are the things you need to feel content in your life. Work is not the only important thing that you will do in your life. It is one of the important things, but it must be squared in a way in which you achieve life-work balance.

A Society of Human Resource Management study previously this millennium found that six in ten (58%) workers stated they wanted their work to provide the flexibility that allowed them to balance their life and work. It was the most sought after workplace trait, one that many believe will keep their career from running or ruining their life.

The print and electronic media are prone to use the term *work-life balance*. This book reverses the terms and, in so doing, places greater emphasis on the larger picture. After all, your workday is not a 24/7 arrangement and what you do at work should be balanced with what you do the rest of your life. They are indelibly connected but need to be considered separately.

The opportunity to have and enjoy leisure time compared with long work hours may be an important lifestyle characteristic for you. Another could be your choice of living in a smaller, more intimate community over a large, busy city. Environmental issues and conservation of natural resources are growing public concerns, ones that many people have come to value highly and have elected to advance in their daily lives. Some individuals welcome work that involves travel and the opportunity to see other places. For just as many others, there is "no place like home." As you move into and through adulthood, these preferences will become important elements in your life, ones that could point you in the direction of the work that you will do.

Identifying the Characteristics that Define You

Many of the personal characteristics cited thus far are easily identifiable or can be measured in some way. Some you can recite without hesitation as you have observed your personal growth and development and the traits that comprise your being. Others can be identified or pointed out by the people close to you (e.g., parents, friends, teachers, etc.). Through the use of interest inventories, aptitude tests, and other assessments, counselors are able to evaluate many of the personal characteristics that might influence your career development. The results of this standardized testing, coupled with your personal assessment and that of others, can assist in creating a personal profile you can use in your career exploration.

Some of the characteristics that you observe now will become entrenched and remain a part of you for life. Additional ones will emerge as you grow, mature, and have more life experiences. The "Who am I?" assessment represents a point in time in your growth and development and will only be valid during the present and immediate future; it is a snapshot of who you are at the moment.

Any exercise in personal analysis is one that should be repeated periodically to ensure that the profile you are creating is current and accurate. As a changing, growing, and dynamic person you will want the best information to make sound educational and career decisions. Be aware of these dynamics, and be diligent in your search for information about yourself.

A word about leadership is appropriate at this time. People who lead and manage in their career roles rarely start out in those types of positions, but their leadership and management traits were likely present at an early age or most certainly early in their career. It is a rare business owner or entrepreneur who begins his or her career in such a role, but the characteristics needed to be a successful businessperson are likely to have existed for a long time. When these characteristics exist and are displayed in an individual, they can often lead to positions of responsibility and authority.

What Tests and Other Instruments Can Tell You
As any explorer navigates the period of self-discovery, professional counselors may be able to recommend, administer, and interpret formal appraisal and measurement instruments that pinpoint the interests, aptitudes, values, traits, and other individual characteristics discussed here. Be careful, however, not to make decisions based on the findings of a single test. Take another assessment or discuss the implications of the findings with a counselor.

Test and inventory findings represent just a piece of who you are. Make certain you understand what each instrument is measuring but also—just as important—what it doesn't measure. The following are a number of the popular assessment instruments:

- Armed Services Vocational Aptitude Battery (www.asvabprogram.com)*
- CareerKey (www.careerkey.org)
- Keirsey Temperament Sorter (www.keirsey.com)*
- Myers-Briggs Type Indicator® (MBTI) (www.myersbriggs.org)
- O*NET Online Job Skills Directory (http://online.onetcenter.org/)*
- Self-Directed Search (www.self-directed-search.com)

Note: A number of the assessments identified have a fee associated with their administration. Check with your counselor before proceeding to determine if the assessment is available via your institution or agency without charge. Those marked with an asterisk (*) are free.

As this self-discovery process is implemented, it is important to follow two rules. The first is to leave no part of you unexamined. The more you know about yourself, the better you will be able to address the "fit" issues that were addressed previously. The second is to remember that you are a dynamic, evolving creature, and any examination of personal characteristics is simply a view of you at this time.

Return periodically to self-assessment and ensure the personal profile you are creating is current and accurate.

Career Fact: Success in Certain Occupations Can Best Be Achieved by Those Possessing Specific Characteristics and Traits
Auditors and accountants must enjoy and be good at crunching numbers. Emergency medical personnel must do their best work in "pressure-filled" situations. Carpenters, electricians, and plumbers must be attentive to detail. Customer service representatives have to possess "people" skills. The list of characteristics and traits needed to function effectively in particular careers and occupations is long and varied. The portrayal of these characteristics, along with the knowledge and skill required to carry out the essential work functions, will take the individual a long way toward career success.

Frequently Asked Questions
Question: Is there a point in time when personal characteristics solidify and stop changing and I am who I am going to be?
Answer: Humans are evolving and changing all the time. Counselors and psychologists believe that most of your personality is shaped by the time you reach late adolescence and young adulthood, but it is not a facet of you that will be cemented forever at this time. New learning and life experiences can extend your awareness and influence your career development from that point forward.

Question: How important is tying what you study to your career ambitions and goals?
Answer: Learning, formal and informal, is a great influence. Almost everything we study in school or college can be relevant to the knowledge, skills, and competencies required in some occupation or career, and probably many of them. As you progress through your educational experiences, pause occasionally to consider the career relevance of the things you are learning and how that learning might be applied in career fields or settings that you are considering.

Question: When a person observes aspects of a career or occupation that appear reasonable, but others that are not as appealing, how can this conflict be resolved?
Answer: First, the conflicts may not be able to be resolved. When the cons far exceed the pros, it is probably a career or occupation that you should steer away from. On the other hand, it may be important to determine what about a particular career detracts you and the extent to which that may be corrected or mitigated. Your "likes," as well as your "dislikes," are part of your psychosocial being. Pay attention to them.

Student Exercise 4.1

The Personal Audit: How Do You See Yourself?

Complete the audit that follows. Review your responses periodically, and update any information that does not reflect your current view of your personal characteristics.

1. Abilities and skills are the talents that you possess. They may have come to the surface in your schoolwork (e.g., conducting research for a term paper, etc.) or in your daily life (e.g., interacting with others in a group, etc.). Others you don't possess now will emerge as you develop and learn. List the abilities and skills you have at this point in your life.

   _____

   _____

2. Aptitudes represent your capacity for learning, your natural ability to do something. They can range from academic things like writing or mathematics to other strengths like music or athletics. Make a list of your strongest aptitudes.

   _____

   _____

3. Achievements are the measured accomplishments of your life, those things that you have done well or those for which you have received recognition. They include things like making the honor roll, setting a record for rebounds in basketball, or collecting the most food for the homeless at Thanksgiving. List the achievements for which you have been recognized.

   _____

   _____

4. Interests are the things you like to do, spend time doing, and arouse your curiosity. Sometimes they are spin-offs of your aptitudes, including things like writing. Other interests may include taking photos, playing the guitar, collecting sport cards, or cooking. Often they are things you do just for fun. List your interests here.

_____

_____

5. Personality traits are those individual characteristics that make you different from other people. Words like *outgoing, quiet, inquisitive*, and *studious* come to mind when thinking of personality traits. List those personal traits.

_____

_____

6. Values are the aspects of your life that matter to you, those you hold in esteem, and the principles that you believe in, stand behind, and would fight to maintain. A commitment to family and friends, loyalty to your school, and your religious beliefs are excellent examples. Write a few of those values.

_____

_____

7. Lifestyle preferences are similar to values but may be just a bit more practical in their application to you personally. They are the things you need to feel content and satisfied. The presence of leisure time compared with long working hours is an example. Another would be your choice of living in a smaller community instead of living in a busy city. Or vice versa. What are some of the things you prefer for your life?

_____

_____

8. What do you consider to be your greatest personal strengths and attributes?

_____

_____

9. What do you consider to be your greatest weaknesses or shortcomings?

_____

_____

10. List three school subjects or interests you would like to continue to study and possibly integrate into your work tasks one day.

   _____

   _____

11. Which school subjects have you enjoyed the most?

   _____

   _____

12. Which school subjects posed the greatest challenges to you?

   _____

   _____

13. Which school subjects have you enjoyed studying the least?

   _____

   _____

14. What school subjects resulted in your poorest grades?

   _____

   _____

15. Identify a recent experience that stimulated your intellectual curiosity or one for which you enjoyed the challenge as exciting and arousing:

   _____

   _____

16. How would you describe your academic performance to date? Is your school record a true reflection of your academic ability or potential? If not, how would you characterize your ability and potential for success in future studies?

   _____

   _____

Student Exercise 4.2

The External Portrait: How Others See You

Make a list of up to five traits or descriptors (e.g., enthusiastic, hard-working, creative, etc.) you feel others would use to describe you. Remember, different people see you in different environments and witness different things about you. Your coach, for example, may see things that your parents don't. If you don't know exactly how others view you, take this opportunity to ask them.

Parents/Family Members:

_____

_____

_____

_____

Teachers/Counselors:

_____

_____

_____

_____

Friends/Fellow Students:

_____

_____

_____

_____

Coaches/Youth Activity Leaders:

_____

_____

_____

_____

Employer/Previous Employers:

_____

_____

_____

_____

Minister/Priest/Rabbi/Religious Leader:

_____

_____

_____

_____

Student Exercise 4.3

Setting Achievable Career Goals

This is an exercise that you can complete and then return to many times as the career development process evolves for you. In the spaces that follow, list the careers that hold particular interest for you, ones that you could see yourself performing one day. List only those careers you believe to be achievable and realistic in terms of what you know about yourself and the careers. Revisit and revise your career goals at any point you learn anything of significance about yourself or the world of work.

Date　　Careers Holding Special Interest for Me

_____

_____

_____

_____

_____

_____

_____

_____

_____

_____

_____

CHAPTER FIVE

~

The Dynamics of
the American Workplace

Past, Present, and Future

> The society which scorns excellence in plumbing as a humble activity
> and tolerates shoddiness in philosophy because it is an exalted activity
> will have neither good plumbing nor good philosophy: neither its pipes
> nor its theories will hold water.
>
> —John W. Gardner, former secretary of Health, Education, and
> Welfare and founder of Common Cause

Readers are probably not expecting a history lesson in a book about exploring
options and choosing a career, but there are some historical considerations
that will help you understand the present and prepare you for the future. If
the working world was static, all that you would need would be a set of occupational descriptors to help you to explore and choose. But it is not, and
what follows is a short treatise on how the existing workplace came to be
and how many of the dynamics of change are a constant influence on work
in the United States.

   An agrarian, agriculturally driven society in its early days, the United States
eventually became an industrial nation in the late part of the nineteenth century. Every imaginable kind of product was made in the factories and mills of
the nation and greatly influenced its occupational structure. The expanse of
manufacturing and production occupations that once drove the US economy
gave way during the latter part of the twentieth century to a workplace that
was driven more by information technology and communication.

Over the nation's history, large numbers of Americans moved from the fields to the factories to the current mix of diversified work environments. Throughout these periods, the workplace has been home to a set of core careers and occupations, including those in health, education, government, and business that respond continuously to the call of all citizens for goods and services.

In chapter 7, you will be introduced to the concept of career clusters (e.g., health and medicine, public service, communications and media, etc.), a series of occupational groupings that are interlaced to form the composite US workforce profile. Some careers have been around seemingly forever, whereas others come and go with changing economic and societal conditions. But even the omnipresent occupations change in some respects, as exemplified by the influences of technology and innovation on the way work is performed.

The nation's population growth over time has been influential because increasing numbers of individuals are needed to provide personal care and services. Larger numbers of people require more teachers, nurses, retail salespeople, engineers, technicians, and the countless others who provide services to and make products for the masses. Although remnants of our agricultural and industrial past remain, the workplace is influenced today significantly by professional, information, technical, and service careers. Demographic trends and the movement of people also have an effect on the workplace, if nothing more than the development of urban and metropolitan centers where a significant portion of US occupations are performed.

US creativity and invention during the last century, a facet of our national character that has continued into the current millennium, brought incredible change to our homes, schools, and the places where we work. Space exploration and the first moonwalk, events that happened in the second half of the last century, are living proof of how innovation and change affected every citizen. Technology has improved our capacity to communicate, influenced productivity and efficiency, and hastened the speed with which we accomplish many life and work tasks. Imagine a world without the Internet, cell phones, digital cameras, and HD television. Your parents can. Your grandparents really can!

A century influenced by world wars, major military conflicts, and a Cold War saw the United States rise to a position of power and influence in the global community. US business and financial structures dominate the manner in which the world does business today. Significant changes in international manufacturing and industrial production emerged toward the end of the century and remain today as issues influencing individuals and the economy. The negative side of the global picture is that many jobs once considered stalwarts in the US workplace have been transitioned to other countries and lost to the US economy.

Work in the United States offers career seekers boundless and varied options. The breadth and number of work opportunities in the United States equals or exceeds those across the globe, a factor that can be viewed both positively and negatively. The good news is there are lots of things that you can do. With greater opportunity comes an even greater challenge. At some point, possibly soon, you will have to work your way through this career and occupational maze, make decisions, and point yourself down a path toward one or a cluster of careers.

Americans respect the dignity of all work and respect the workers who perform the myriad roles that constitute the US workforce. Yes, we have some who separate work into "white collar" and "blue collar" and maybe even associate a certain classism with the categories, but collectively our nation places a high value on quality whether one is making a product or performing a service. Those who view work through a hierarchical lens, believing that some career or work is more important than others, need to reread the John W. Gardner quote that introduces this chapter. Failure to respect all work and all workers results in a division or separation of people according to an occupational status that is misplaced in the socioeconomic structure of our nation.

The Influence of the Economy and World Events on the Workplace

Many of the factors that helped shape the US occupational structure in the latter portion of the twentieth century have continued as influential factors in the current millennium. In general, job growth remained steady after 2000 until a slowing emerged in 2007 and a decline appeared in 2008, brought on by a downturn in the economy and a recession. Since 2008, the Department of Labor has reported a steady increase in the number of Americans working and record lows in unemployment.

The reality of job loss and lack of opportunity, however, remain a sobering threat to many US workers. The impact of 9/11, threats of other terrorist acts, military conflicts in various parts of the world, and global events such as the coronavirus outbreak in 2020 are believed by many historians and economists to impact the economy, and their full effect on the workplace has been the subject of considerable debate. Although the specific impact of world and national events is often difficult to assess, they are worthy of constant monitoring. All Americans should regularly take the pulse of global and national trends because they are likely to influence both work and workers.

Relationship of Education to Work in the United States

Many elements of the US workplace have been influenced by education and educational attainment. As this is expected to continue, the following factors are worthy of consideration by career explorers:

- Although "high school" and "high school/some college" occupations still account for most jobs in the United States, high job growth and high wage growth occupations are associated with greater levels of post-secondary educational attainment (e.g., bachelor's, master's, doctoral, and first professional degrees).
- Education pays. The median weekly earnings of US workers in 2007 in relation to their level of educational attainment was as follows: Less than high school diploma: $553; high school graduate: $730; some college, no degree: $802: associate degree: $812; bachelor's degree: $1,198; graduate/professional degree: $1,659; and doctoral degree: $1,835.
- Employment of Americans can be directly correlated with levels of educational attainment. The greater the achievement, the lower the unemployment level: Less than high school diploma: 5.6 percent; high school graduate: 4.1 percent; some college, no degree: 3.7 percent; associate degree: 2.8 percent; bachelor's degree: 2.2 percent; graduate/professional degree: 1.8 percent; and doctoral degree: 1.6 percent (2020).
- Education impacts unemployment because individuals with lower educational attainment are more likely to be unemployed. The cost of not completing high school is felt in both earnings and job security.

Relevance of Workforce Statistics for Explorers

What do statistics like this tell us about the composition of the US workforce and what is the relevance of this information for career explorers? First, it is important for those looking forward to understand the general composition of the US workplace. The statistics represent the "playing field" on which you will eventually work. They tell us something about change that has occurred, is occurring, and is likely to emerge in the US workplace of tomorrow.

Finally, a careful review of the numbers suggests areas of diminishing need and obsolescence.

Following are some of the most significant findings reflected in the contemporary workforce statistics:

- By their size, the more populated occupations (e.g., salesperson, teacher, nurse, etc.) represent greater opportunity for career seekers and changers. But even while suggesting numerical growth in the coming decade, a significant number of large occupations (e.g., business and office workers, manufacturing workers, etc.) may be on the "endangered species" list—meaning they could become obsolete or in less demand than before.

- Innovation and technology are influencing the emergence of new occupations and affecting the numbers required to fill many existing positions. Such change represents a double-edged sword as the technology that takes occupations away from the workforce is also responsible for the creation of new ones.

- Population and demographic shifts, including the "graying" of the baby-boomer generation and the increased life expectancy of seniors, have been influential in the larger numbers of positions in health, medical, and social service settings. The growing demand for services in these environments is driving the number of positions up.

- The decline in many production, distribution, and related occupations has been influenced by the movement of much of that work to offshore locations in the latter part of the last century. Other manufacturing careers have been affected by major technological advances such as robotics and the movement—called offshoring—to places where products can be produced less expensively. Any decline in office and administrative occupations can be traced to changes brought on by the new technologies and the emergence of new protocols such as telecommuting, decentralization of operations, and other business innovations.

- Many of the statistics produce a "crystal ball" effect, allowing the consumer to predict future trends in the US workplace by explaining "what's hot" and "what's not." Health care and the provision of social and mental health services dominate recent Department of Labor projections of the fastest-growing occupations. Other sectors expected to grow include occupations that address issues of financial well-being and the demand for sophisticated information technologies and efficient communication systems, often referred to as the STEM (science, technology, engineering, and mathematics) careers, as well as the new ways (i.e., eCommerce) in which sales and distribution fulfillment (i.e., packages delivered by drones) are conducted today.

Note: Career explorers will find the *Occupational Outlook Handbook* of the US Bureau of Labor Statistics a valuable source of demographic trends about the US workplace. Visit http://stats.bls.gov/oco regularly to access this information.

Changes to Workplace Settings and Protocols

Remember the passage previously in this book about the percentage of people who will enter occupations that didn't exist when they started school. Not only will many careers be new and different, but the way they and other traditional careers are performed will also change. Consider the changes that have and will continue to occur in the workplace settings and protocols:

- Traditional work structures like the forty-hour workweek are giving way to flexible schedules. In your grandparent's day, the majority of Americans worked 9 a.m. to 5 p.m., Monday through Friday. Many manufacturing locations divided the forty-hour workweek in eight-hour shifts to maximize production capacity. The same is true of those facilities like hospitals, fire and police departments, and others that have to be accessible and functional around the clock. During the time your parents have been in the workforce, a number of innovations and experiments with work schedules have resulted in different and more flexible work calendars for many people.
- Increasing numbers of people are engaged in telecommuting or teleworking and currently perform their work roles from home or a neutral work location that is connected to their primary employer through the use of information technology. Attempted initially as a procedure that would allow working parents to function from home and tend to childcare responsibilities, telecommuting was discovered to be an effective alternative to assembling large numbers of people into an office or related environment. This feature is viewed as a "win-win" adjustment. Workers enjoy the freedom and flexibility of working in this manner, employers have been able to eliminate or reduce costs for space, infrastructure, and overhead.
- Innovations like job sharing where two individuals hold part of one full-time position or each work two-thirds time offer value to both the worker and the employer, thus creating yet another innovation that is pleasing to both the employee and the employer. I recall an ad posted by a college for a half-time biology professor/half-time literature professor that encouraged wife and husband applications and promised to create teaching schedules that would accommodate both working parents

if they wanted to make certain childcare schedules were covered. This represents yet another example of employer flexibility.

- A growing entrepreneurial spirit and desire for many professional services to work independently is resulting in a greater number of small, start-up firms across the spectrum of the US workforce. Additionally, many women and men are electing to perform their roles as part of an "outsourced" or contract relationship with the firm, organization, or agency needing their service.

- The United States is doing its business differently than it did in your grandparent's day. An excellent example is the brewing industry that was dominated by large (i.e., Anheuser-Busch, Coors, Millers, etc.) firms in the latter part of the last century. Today, those firms are experiencing mega competition from smaller, craft breweries that have sprung up in varied places around the country and offer employment in varied positions in a different, often more desirable, business framework from the larger companies.

- Environmentalists see a four-day workweek that has been adopted in many work environments as reducing the worker commute by 20 percent and impacting both the amount of gasoline being consumed and emissions in the air. As a result, many businesses, agencies, and organizations are introducing a "green" day once or twice a month.

- A host of life-work balance issues are getting attention. Yes, employers want the old-fashioned loyalty and commitment that has been a hallmark of the US workplace for years. But the twenty-first century innovations mentioned here have shown that quality performance by employees can be achieved along with a greater response to their life-work balance desires. Flexibility in how one performs an occupational role has become a reward that many are pleased to accept in place of greater remuneration. By accepting alternative ways of achieving a goal or seeing work through to completion, the contemporary business, agency, or organization is helping its workforce achieve that balance. Watch for additional changes of this nature in the future.

Inside the Numbers: Selected Career Statistics Explorers Should Know
Your brain could become numb reading the pages and pages of statistics that the US Department of Labor, Census Bureau, and professional and trade associations have generated about the workforce and opportunities that exist there now and in the future. This guidebook has selected a number of those lists that contain information that is worthy of examination.

Careers and Occupations that Employ the Most Americans
Reason to Know: These twenty-five occupations employ the greatest number of people in the United States, and each consistently has both growth and replacement opportunities.

1. Retail salespersons
2. Food preparation and service workers
3. Cashiers
4. Office clerks
5. Registered nurses
6. Customer service representative
7. Laborers and freight and stock movers
8. Waiters and waitresses
9. Personal care aides
10. Janitors and cleaners (not maids and housekeepers)
11. Secretaries, administrative and personal assistants
12. General and operations managers
13. Stock clerks and order fillers
14. Truck drivers, heavy and tractor-trailer
15. Bookkeeping, accounting, and auditing clerks
16. First-line supervisors of office and administrative workers
17. First-line supervisor of retail workers
18. Nursing assistants
19. Maids and housekeepers
20. Maintenance and repair workers
21. Elementary school teachers, except special education
22. Accountants and auditors
23. Sales representatives, wholesale and manufacturing
24. Construction laborers
25. Teaching assistants

Note: This list mainly represents occupations that require the basic knowledge and skill set offered in career and occupational training programs. As career positions move up the occupational ladder or lattice, so do the education and experience requirements.

Career and Occupational Groups Projected for the Greatest Growth (Present–2028)
Reason to Know: As families or clusters of careers and occupations, these popular fields are expected to grow at a pace that exceeds others. A number

of these groups will grow because of their emergence in the contemporary US workplace. Others will become larger because of a growing population, one that is living longer and healthier lives.

1. Professional and related occupations
2. Service occupations
3. Information technology and communication exchange occupations
4. Health and medical occupations
5. Office and administrative support occupations
6. Sales, marketing, distribution, and related occupations
7. Personal care occupations
8. Management, business, and financial occupations
9. Electronic commerce and distribution occupations
10. Hospitality, leisure time, and recreation occupations
11. Education, preschool through higher education occupations, including distance learning
12. Transportation and materials moving occupations
13. Construction and extraction occupations
14. Installation, maintenance, and repair occupations

Fastest-Growing Careers and Occupations (Present–2028)
Reason to Know: Each of these careers and occupations reflects areas of growth and need as dictated greatly by the issues of technology and service (e.g., personal, health, and social). Innovation and changing business practices can results in adjustments to this list at any time.

1. Personal care aides
2. Combined food preparation and serving workers, including fast food
3. Registered nurses
4. Home health aides
5. Cooks, restaurant
6. Software developers, applications
7. Waiters and waitresses
8. General and operations managers
9. Janitors and cleaners, except maids and housekeeping cleaners
10. Medical technicians and assistants
11. Construction laborers
12. Laborers and freight, stock, and material movers, hand
13. Market research analysts and marketing specialists
14. Nursing assistants

15. Management analysts
16. First-line supervisors of food preparation and serving workers
17. Landscaping workers and groundskeepers
18. Financial managers
19. Heavy and tractor-trailer truck drivers
20. Medical secretaries

Fastest-Growing Careers and Occupations for Degree Achievers with the Highest Percentage Change of Employment (Present–2028)
Reason to Know: People who have college study as their educational goal should know the careers and occupations that are the fastest growing for degree achievers. Visit the *Occupational Outlook Handbook* site (https://www.bls.gov/ooh) of the US Department of Labor to learn more about positions with which you are unfamiliar.

1. Solar photovoltaic installers
2. Wind turbine service technicians
3. Home health aides
4. Occupational therapy assistants
5. Information security analysts
6. Physician assistants
7. Statisticians
8. Nurse practitioners
9. Speech-language pathologists
10. Physical therapist assistants
11. Genetic counselors
12. Mathematicians
13. Operations research analysts
14. Software developers, applications
15. Forest fire inspectors and prevention specialists
16. Health specialties teachers, postsecondary
17. Phlebotomists
18. Physical therapist aides
19. Medical assistants
20. Cybersecurity specialists

Careers and Occupations with Largest Number of Openings for College Graduates
Reason to Know: People interested in studying at the college level and meeting the degree requirements for the bachelor's degree will benefit from know-

ing the careers and occupations with the largest number of openings awaiting them on completion of their studies.

1. General and operations managers
2. Registered nurses
3. Accountants and auditors
4. Business operations managers and specialists
5. Elementary school teachers, except special education
6. Management analysts
7. Software developers, applications
8. Managers, all other types
9. Market research analysts and research specialists
10. Secondary school teachers
11. Substitute teachers
12. Human resources managers
13. Financial managers
14. Computer systems analysts
15. Middle school teachers
16. Coaches and scouts
17. Behavior disorders, substance abuse, and mental health counselors
18. Buyers and purchasing agents
19. Construction managers
20. Sales managers
21. Training and development specialists
22. Child, family, and school social workers
23. Sales representatives, wholesale and manufacturing
24. Computer specialists, all others
25. Software developers, systems

Careers and Occupations Projected to Have the Largest Number of Openings as a Result of Growth and Need for Replacements (Present–2025)
Reason to Know: These careers and occupations employ large numbers of people and continue to be ones that have strong growth and replacement needs.

1. Retail salespersons
2. Combined food preparation and serving workers, including fast food
3. Cashiers
4. Waiters and waitresses
5. Registered nurses

6. Customer service representatives
7. Janitors and cleaners, except maids and housekeepers
8. Personal care aides and assistants
9. General and operational managers
10. Nursing assistants
11. Home health aides
12. Secretaries and administrative assistants
13. Childcare workers
14. Stock clerks and order fillers
15. Accountants and auditors
16. First-line supervisors of office and administrative workers
17. Construction laborers
18. Maids and housekeepers
19. Elementary school teachers, except special education
20. Heavy and tractor-trailer truck drivers
21. Landscaping workers and groundskeepers
22. Sales representatives, wholesaled and manufacturing
23. First-line supervisor of retail workers
24. Receptionists and information clerks
25. Teaching assistants

Careers and Occupations Projected to Have the Largest Employment Decline (Present–2025)
Reason to Know: These careers and occupations are most likely to be affected by systems innovation, technology, robotics, and other issues that result in position loss and obsolescence.

1. Stock clerks and order fillers
2. Cashiers
3. Postal service managers and workers
4. Data entry and word-processing clerks
5. File clerks
6. Machine operators and support workers
7. Assemblers
8. Telemarketers
9. Farm, ranch, and agricultural managers and workers
10. Travel agents and transportation support workers

Note: The information presented in the various lists is found in the occupational reports generated by the Bureau of Labor Statistics of the US

Department of Labor, US Census Bureau, and varied professional and trade organizations.

To say the US workplace has been in a state of evolution would be an understatement. An examination of the nation's most recent history will help the observer understand and appreciate the adjustments that have been made by US business, including up and down periods, a dot.com boom and subsequent bust, and economic prosperity followed by the throes of a recession and then recovery. Awareness of these trends and events can lead to sound personal decisions.

Career Myth: The United States Is the Land of Opportunity, and There Are Always Occupations that Are Open for People Who Wish to Work

The US workplace offers a fantastic array, as well as an enormous number of different careers and occupations. That is not to say, however, that the supply and demand for people in many of those positions will not be affected by economic and business conditions. Periods of recession and economic downturn affect people who are working, and some will lose their positions to downsizing and reductions in force (RIF). Those same conditions have a negative impact on individuals in school or college and preparing to be new entrants to the workforce. These situations dictate that occupation holders and those seeking to enter occupations keep abreast of manpower trends and statistics and use this information to their personal benefit.

Frequently Asked Questions

Question: How important should the total size of a career or occupation be to me as I consider my options?

Answer: The number of people employed in a career or occupation can be influential in a number of ways. Consider the occupations of astronomer and science professor, for instance. The smaller numbers of astronomers will impact clearly supply and demand. There are far more opportunities for science professors. Lesser populated occupations may also impact where positions will be found. Astronomers, as an example, tend to be employed in areas that have universities, laboratories, or observatories. Science professors, on the other hand, will find greater numbers of career opportunities in far many more settings and environments.

Question: What are the factors that are driving so many of the changes in how work is performed?

Answer: A number of things have influenced the new and different ways people perform their work, including a desire to control costs and respond to the needs of employees. Telecommuting, for example, drives down the need for office space and related costs as employees work from home or remote locations. Flexible hours and position sharing are worker-friendly strategies that contribute to life-work balance and have become popular with employees and led to improved retention rates. Finally, telecommuting and modified or shortened workweeks are seen as environmentally conscious policies as fewer community workers are using fuel and polluting the air.

Question: How important is having a college degree to my being successful in the workplace?

Answer: The fact that most of the work performed in the United States still does not require a college degree is one that has changed of late and will likely change more in the future. It is reasonable to assume that all of the professional and technical-, trade-, and career-oriented occupations will require some level of study beyond high school. It may be an apprenticeship or a certificate program at a community, junior, or technical college. Many of the new careers and occupations demand more education and preparation, and individuals still in school should set goals that allow them to achieve their full educational and career potential. That would be the safest and surest path to the world of work.

Student Exercise 5.1

Career Familiarity: Current and Future

1. In the space provided, list the careers and occupations with which you have a high degree of familiarity but ones that you only need to monitor as you proceed through the exploration process.

   _____

   _____

   _____

2. In the space provided, list the careers and occupations with which you have some degree of familiarity but ones that you wish to examine in greater detail as you proceed through the exploration process.

   _____

   _____

   _____

3. In the space provided, list the careers and occupations with which you have little or no familiarity, ones that hold interest for you but will require more extensive study or research as you proceed through the exploration process.

   _____

   _____

   _____

CHAPTER SIX

~

Strategies for Learning about the World of Work

We learn 10 percent of what we read, 20 percent of what we hear, 30 percent of what we see, 50 percent of what we see and hear, 70 percent of what we discuss and 80 percent of what we experience.

—William Glaser, MD, educator and counseling theorist

Unless you expect to win your state lottery or inherit the kind of wealth that will allow you to never set foot in the US workplace, a career is destined to appear somewhere in your future. The more you know about careers, coupled with what has been presented already in this book about what you need to know about yourself, the more you will be helped in making optimal choices, ones that will lead to comfort and success for you and a sound investment for your eventual employer.

The United States affords career explorers a huge number of options. That number will shrink rapidly, however, as you learn more about yourself and your goals and begin to pass the various occupations through a personal filter. Remaining will be a number of occupations or careers that should be the subject of even more focused examination. That study can help identify the career where you will spend a significant portion of your working life.

It is possible that you think you know what you want to do in the future right now. You may be right, but that is all the more reason why a thorough examination of the larger list of occupations and careers should be something you perform. If the preferred occupation stands up to the added scrutiny, it will validate the position you now hold.

Look at careers like you are looking into a mirror. Is that you flying that plane, surveying that acreage as a potential building site, or performing an operation on that patient? Are you willing to move to the West Coast or Pacific Northwest, where so many of the information technology and computer systems jobs are located? Does the pressure of meeting deadlines in a field like journalism really mesh well with your personality?

To get the answers to these and similar questions, you must acquire as much knowledge as you can about the world of work. Presently, that knowledge is limited. Over time it will grow as education and life experiences expose you to more opportunities and a whole lot more information. It is also a time to be cautious because too much information consumed too fast can result in "information overload."

Role of Information in Career Exploration

Information is essential to decision making and serves three functions in the career development process:

- Information answers questions.
- Information corrects and adjusts misinformation and myths.
- Information motivates.

By far the greatest use of information in career development is the answering of questions. As we learn characteristics about ourselves, it is natural to inquire and connect that knowledge to careers and occupations. This requires the discipline of searching for answers from reliable sources and then using what is learned to set realistic goals and make quality decisions.

The corrective and adjustment function is a bit more complex. As people pass through life, they are exposed to an incredible amount of bad information. Some of it is outdated and no longer relevant. Some of it advances myths and misunderstandings commonly held by people. It wasn't too far back in US history when gender discrimination was present in the workplace and many occupations were considered off limits to women. Some of those biases and stereotypes remain in our society, and good information serves to correct and adjust.

Finally, information has a motivational function. The more people learn about the world of work, the more they want to learn. Answers generate more questions. When known decisions appear in career and education paths, their sheer presence can send the decision maker off on a search to grow and learn and become equipped to choose the best option.

Extending Your Antenna

People are engaged in careers all around you. Imagine the working people that you can reach out and touch. They are the teachers and professors in the classroom; the police officers, firefighters, and emergency medical service professionals responsible for our safety and security; the healthcare providers in all of the various departments at the local hospital; and the managers, clerks, and service providers in all of the businesses and firms in the community. They are everyday people performing seemingly routine roles in the varied institutions, businesses, firms, agencies, and organizations that comprise the US work enterprise. They are everywhere, and you need to adjust your personal antenna to pick up the informational signals each is sending.

Some of the members of the workforce are more visible than others. You see many because you encounter them as they perform their roles or seek the products and services they provide. Some you meet face-to-face. Others you see on television or read about in newspapers. The visible workers that you encounter are individuals like the teacher, professor, dental hygienist, police officer, nurse, pilot, television actress/actor, and bank teller. Because of their visible presence in our lives, our antennas need not work hard to connect us to them and display what they do.

Other workers, similar in ways to an Antarctic iceberg, are less visible to us. The tip of the iceberg is visible, but its mass is not. The world of work is similar. You don't typically see the architect, but you see the homes, schools, office buildings, and other structures that each designs. You don't see the journalists, but you read the newspaper or weekly newsmagazine containing their work. You don't see the medical analysts studying your tests and records, but your physician depends upon their work to diagnose and treat you.

They, and countless others, are the behind-the-scenes professionals, skilled workers, technicians, and support personnel whose importance is major but whose visibility is either negligible or nonexistent. Your antenna will have to work much harder to allow you to see the entire iceberg.

Life Experiences as Career Teachers

There are a variety of ways in which you can learn about careers, including:

- **Casual observation.** As a casual observer of people and what they do in the workplace, you are learning about careers and occupations. These informal observations can be packed full of good information, and the lessons learned will help guide you in choosing your personal career one day.

Student Exercise 6.1

Career Visibility Survey: How Many Can You See?

1. Identify the careers or occupations you have personally observed in the last day, several days, or week. List them here.

   _____

   _____

   _____

2. Think about the experiences you have had over the past few days and determine what "invisible" people in what careers caused those things to happen. Example: Did you see a newly released movie over the weekend? What careers and occupations helped to create and bring you that film? List them here.

   _____

   _____

   _____

Student Exercise 6.2

Preparing for the Career Shadowing Experience

Career/Occupation Site: _____ Contact Person: _____
Telephone: _____ E-mail address: _____
Date of visit: _____ Time: _____

Career observers and interviewers get the most out of each "shadowing" experience when they plan what they wish to do and prepare questions in advance. What do you want to learn? What do you want to see and do? You might ask about the range of different occupations that are performed in the setting, how people prepare educationally to enter those occupations, and what kinds of work tasks are performed by individuals on a typical day. Avoid personal questions like how much an individual earns. Be prepared to follow up during the interview because answers to questions spawn new ones.

Some career visits will afford a unique opportunity to tour the office or facility and see the instruments and tools of that workplace (e.g., television studio). Some may even provide a hands-on exposure during the visit. Determine in advance if these types of activities are a possibility.

Questions for individual(s) performing career/occupation:

_____

_____

_____

Things you want to see and experiences you would like to have during your visit:

_____

_____

_____

Note: Make additional copies of this form for each career and occupation setting visit.

Student Exercise 6.3

Evaluating the Career Shadowing Experience

Rate your impression of the following career- and work-related elements as experienced or observed during each "shadowing" experience. Circle the number that best reflects your impression. If other features influenced you favorably or unfavorably, list each in the vacant spaces and rate it. Check "DNO" ("did not observe") if you are unable to evaluate an element.

Career/Occupation Setting:

	Favorable				Unfavorable	
Work climate/culture/atmosphere	5	4	3	2	1	DNO
Staff spirit and enthusiasm	5	4	3	2	1	DNO
Friendliness and geniality	5	4	3	2	1	DNO
Appearance of work environment	5	4	3	2	1	DNO
Size of operation/mix of people	5	4	3	2	1	DNO
Location of workplace	5	4	3	2	1	DNO
Other	5	4	3	2	1	
_____	5	4	3	2	1	
_____	5	4	3	2	1	
_____	5	4	3	2	1	
Summary	5	4	3	2	1	

Note: Make additional copies of this form for each visit.

CHAPTER SEVEN

~

Mounting a Career Search

Asking the Right Questions

If you're happy in what you're doing, you'll like yourself, you'll have inner peace. And . . . you will have more success than you could possibly have imagined.

—Johnny Carson, entertainer and thirty-year host of *The Tonight Show*

It is time to step up the career search process. In the previous chapter, you learned some of the casual and informal ways of learning about work and the workplace. Now it's time to become more assertive—to turn up the heat—to mount an assertive career search or information campaign.

Two considerations must be part of mounting an effective search. First, as effective exploration will make apparent, many thousands of occupations comprise the US workforce. Equally relevant is the projection that the average US worker will spend between thirty-five and forty years of his or her life in that workforce. This is simply too long to be doing something that isn't right for you or something that doesn't bring you the rewards, satisfaction, and inner peace you desire. The goal of your exploration should be to maximize the chances that you are making the best career "fit."

Mounting an effective career search means asking lots of questions, but they have to be the right questions and you cannot give up until you get the answers. What you learn will make you a better decision maker. The better job you do in this research endeavor, the more likely you will be to understand the range of viable options that lie before you.

Research Areas Guaranteed to Produce Career Knowledge
Often students become interested in a specific career or occupation early in life and use the adolescent and young adult years to affirm that interest. These students learn enough to support their continued movement in that career direction, or they discard the notion as one that is, although interesting and attractive on the surface, probably not worthy of additional pursuit. Other students move into the latter years of school with nothing more than a faint interest in specific careers or a general interest in many careers, both characteristics that demand focused exploration and lots of asking questions.

Whether you elect to interview people in the workplace to learn more about their career or approach your search like a research project in the library or on the Internet, there are eleven "core" research areas that will help you create a profile for any career you are examining. Don't rest until you have gotten answers to each of the questions, and remember that many occupations with the same title are performed in a variety of work settings. Each could generate a slightly different profile.

The eleven research areas that should guide your study of careers and occupations include the following:

1. Nature or role definition: What is the general nature of the work? What are the duties or responsibilities of people performing this career?
2. Settings where work is performed: In what work environments (e.g., hospitals, educational institutions, retail outlets, manufacturing centers, etc.) are you most likely to find this career? Is this a career that could be performed in a telecommuting arrangement?
3. Worker characteristics and traits: What are the individual characteristics or personality traits most commonly associated with people who perform this career?
4. Location: Are career positions more likely to be found in a concentrated region (e.g., southeastern states, California's Silicon Valley, etc.) or in a particular community type (e.g., urban, rural, university setting, etc.) of the country or dispersed throughout the country?
5. Education and training: What are the traditional or typical educational paths to this career? Can you prepare for entry through any other route?
6. Supply and demand: How much competition (current or future) exists for people in this career?
7. Subject to change: Is this a volatile career and more subject to change than others? How will technology impact people in this career in both the short term and long term?

8. Credentials and requirements: Does this career have any special requirements (e.g., licensing or certification, physical strength, education attainment level, etc.)?

9. Compensation: How are people in this career compensated? Beyond salary and benefits, does this career present any unique benefits (e.g., travel opportunity, on-the-job training, etc.)?

10. Opportunities for career development, growth, and mobility: Will meritorious achievements and length of service (seniority) result in both tangible and intangible benefits?

11. Related careers: What careers and occupations are similar to this one? Who do people in this career interface with on a regular basis?

Several hundred career profiles or descriptions have been prepared according to an outline similar to this one and are contained in the online edition of the *Occupational Outlook Handbook* of the US Department of Labor Bureau of Labor Statistics. Career explorers will find this valuable resource at: http://www.bls.gov/ooh/.

Put Career Information to the Test

As an information consumer, you must evaluate what your research reveals to make certain it is accurate, current, and free of bias of any sort. The age of a piece of career information, for example, can be its greatest enemy. In chapter 8, strategies for use in the evaluation of career information will be presented. Obtaining a backup or second source is always a wise idea, especially if something you have learned doesn't seem right. People actively working in the occupation, for example, or professional counselors can also serve as sounding boards when questions arise.

When you have conducted a thorough career examination and received answers to all of your questions, a true picture of the career or occupation is likely to emerge. It will present a view of the career, how one gets to it, and what it will be like once there. This knowledge is essential to quality career decision making.

The Career Cluster Approach to Career Exploration

One of the techniques used by some career explorers is to focus not on a particular occupation—physician, engineer, journalist, or medical technician—but rather on a cluster of occupations or a grouping of occupations in a particular work setting. Following is a list of the twenty career clusters originally developed by the US Department of Education and refined by other organizations and agencies that group hundreds of different occupations into clusters. After a brief focus statement, you will find a sampling of the representative occupations found in the cluster.

Advertising, Marketing, and Public Relations
> Focus: Careers encompassing the preparation, management, and delivery of information about products and services, including both for-profit and not-for-profit organizations.
>
> Representative occupations: Advertising director, commercial artist, image consultant, graphic designer, market analyst, media representative, opinion pollster, publicist, and technical writer.

Agriculture, Food, and Natural Resources
> Focus: Careers involving the production, processing, marketing, distribution, financing, and development of agricultural commodities and resources, including food, fiber, wood products, natural resources, horticulture, and other plant and animal products and resources.
>
> Representative occupations: Agricultural engineer, agroscience educator, agroforestry research specialist, agronomist, blacksmith, commodity broker, crop duster, farmer, livestock production manager, and soil scientist.

Architecture, Building, and Construction
> Focus: Careers associated with designing, planning, managing, building, and maintaining the built environment.
>
> Representative occupations: Architect, building engineer, building inspector, carpenter, civil engineer construction engineer, electrician, heating and ventilation technician, landscape architect, plumber/pipefitter, and surveyor.

Arts, Entertainment, and Humanities
> Focus: Careers involving the creation, production, exhibition, and performance of multimedia content, including the visual and performing arts and entertainment.
>
> Representative occupations: Actor, actress, artist, camera operator, cinematographer, choreographer, conductor, director, lighting technician, musician, photographer, producer, publicist, and sound technician.

Banking, Finance, and Investments
> Focus: Careers associated with all forms of money management, including banking, borrowing, insurance, and investment.
>
> Representative occupations: Accountant, actuary, auditor, bank manager, broker, controller, consumer loan manager, investment advisor, mortgage loan processor, real estate appraiser, securities analyst, and teller.

Business, Management, and Administration

Focus: Careers addressing the planning, organizing, directing, and evaluating of business functions essential to efficient and productive business operations. Business, management, and administrative careers are found in every sector of the economy.

Representative occupations: Accountant, administrative assistant, auditor, business machine technician, chief executive officer, chief financial officer, customer service representative, entrepreneur/independent business owner, human resources director, office manager, and systems analyst.

Communications and Media

Focus: Careers involving the development and transmittal of print, audio, visual, and related messages and images to a large body of readers, viewers, and listeners.

Representative occupations: Broadcast technician, camera operator, cartoonist, editor, interpreter, newspaper reporter, photographer, proofreader, television/radio reporter, sound/audio technician, videographer, and writer.

Education and Training

Focus: Careers associated with the planning, managing, and providing of education and training services in schools, colleges, workplaces, and related sectors, and related learning support services.

Representative occupations: Distance learning developer, English as a second language (ESL) educator, instructional assistant, librarian/media specialist, principal, professor, psychometrician, school counselor, school psychologist, and teacher.

Environment

Focus: Careers encompassing the array of environmental concerns, dealing with quality of life, conservation, and use of resources.

Representative occupations: Air quality scientist, demographer, forester, forestry technician, geologist, meteorologist, oceanographer, park ranger, soil scientist, and water treatment plant operator.

Government and Public Administration

Focus: Careers involved in the execution of government functions, including governance, national security, foreign services, planning, revenue, and taxation, regulations, and the management of local, state, and federal agencies and programs.

Representative occupations: Assessor, cartographer, city/town manager, city manager, civil engineer, demographer, economist, foreign service officer, home economist, judge, librarian, mental health counselor, military officer, noncommissioned military specialist, postal worker, public health officer, and urban planner.

Health and Medicine

Focus: Careers involving the planning, managing, and providing of therapeutic services, diagnostic services, health informatics, and health support services, as well as biotechnology research and development.

Representative occupations: Audiologist, biochemist, biomedical engineer, dental hygienist, dentist, dietitian, electroencephalogram (EEG) technician, electrocardiogram (ECG) technician, epidemiologist, health services administrator, hospital administrator, laboratory technician, medical assistant, medical illustrator, medical librarian, medical technician, nurse, optician, optometrist, orderly, pharmacist, physician, physician's assistant, physical therapist, podiatrist, radiological technician, rehabilitation counselor, and surgeon.

Hospitality, Leisure, and Tourism

Focus: Careers encompassing the management, marketing, and operation of restaurant and other food services, lodging, tourist attractions, recreational facilities/events, and other tourist-related services.

Representative occupations: Athletic (e.g., golf, tennis, etc.) professional, camp director, chef, curator, flight attendant, hotel manager, maître d', museum educator, personal trainer, recreational director, tour director/guide, and travel agent.

Human and Social Services

Focus: Careers involving the provision of individual and group services in response to human and social needs and requirements.

Representative occupations: Anthropologist, career counselor, day care director, marriage and family therapist, priest/minister/rabbi, psychologist, senior care director, social worker, and youth activity director.

Information Technology

Focus: Careers associated with information technology operations, including technical and professional careers in design, development, support, and management of hardware, software, and systems integration services.

Representative occupations: Computer engineer, computer equipment technician, data entry technician, data miner, IT technician, programmer, systems engineer, and webmaster/designer.

Law, Safety, and Security
Focus: Careers involving the planning, managing, and providing of legal, public safety services, protective services, and homeland security, including professional and support service.

Representative occupations: Alcohol, Tobacco, and Firearms (ATF) agent, Central Intelligence Agency (CIA) agent, corrections officer, court stenographer, crime scene investigator, emergency medical technician, Federal Bureau of Investigation (FBI) agent, firefighter, forensic scientist, paralegal assistant, police officer, security officer, US customs agent, and warden.

Manufacturing and Industry
Focus: Careers associated with the planning, managing, and performing of the processing of materials into intermediate or final products and related professional and support activities such as production planning and control, maintenance, and manufacturing/process engineering.

Representative occupations: Assembler, ceramic engineer, chemist, designer, distribution manager, equipment operator/technician, industrial engineer, machinist, manufacturing engineer, mechanical engineer, metallurgist, millwright, occupational health/safety inspector, pattern maker, quality control engineer, production manager, purchasing agent, safety engineer, test technician, and tool and die maker.

Personal Services
Focus: Careers involving the delivery of services directly to individuals or in support of their personal or lifestyle needs.

Representative occupations: Attorney, caterer, counselor, florist, hairstylist, interior decorator, mortician, personal trainer, realtor, veterinarian, and veterinary technician.

Sales, Service, and Distribution
Focus: Careers encompassing the planning, managing, and performing of sales and marketing activities, including all aspects of customer or consumer service.

Representative occupations: Advertising representative, cashier, credit analyst/officer, customer service representative, inventory control specialist, purchasing agent, retail/wholesale facility manager, and retail/wholesale salesperson.

Science, Technology, Engineering, and Mathematics

Focus: Careers associated with the planning, managing, and providing of scientific research and professional and technical services (e.g., physical science, social science, engineering, etc.), including laboratory and testing services and research and development services.

Representative occupations: Actuary, anthropologist, astronaut, astronomer, biologist, botanist, chemist, entomologist, geographer, geophysicist, laboratory technician, mathematician, meteorologist, research scientist, and technical writer.

Transportation and Logistics

Focus: Careers involving the planning, management, and movement of people, materials, and goods by road, pipeline, air, rail, and water and related professional and technical support services such as transportation infrastructure planning and management, logistics services, and mobile equipment and facility maintenance.

Representative occupations: Aeronautical engineer, airport facility manager, air traffic controller, cartographer, chauffeur, dispatcher, distribution engineer, driver, flight attendant, flight operations director, inventory analyst, navigator, pilot, safety engineer, shipping director, Transportation Security Administration (TSA) agent, and warehouse manager.

Note: The focus definitions are adapted from and used with the permission of the States' Career Cluster Initiative, 2009, www.careertech.org.

Do not consider the preceding groupings to be an exhaustive list of occupations for the cluster. They are merely representative of the mix of occupations that are performed in these fields and settings. Your personal research is certain to discover many more.

Relevance of Work Environment or Setting

Another consideration for some explorers could be the environment or setting in which people work. Individuals with specific occupational skills—accounting, writing, information technology, management, research—can perform those skills in a variety of work environments or settings. Take, for example, the college campus as a work environment. The most visible careers found at most colleges and universities are that of professor, but the teaching occupations represent only a small percentage of the various occupational roles that can be found on the typical college campus.

Some people perform similar career roles in different places. Many accountants, for example, are part of a large cadre of accounting specialists working for a government agency like the Internal Revenue Service (IRS). Other accountants might be members of a smaller team employed by a bank or retail firm. Still others may elect to open a business or tax preparation service and function alone and independently. Each is called an accountant, but the environment, and very likely, their job description, will vary depending on the position and locale.

Following are examples of some of the settings where many careers and occupations are performed:

- Banking and financial centers
- Business centers
- Factories and warehouses
- Government agencies and military installations
- Hospitals and healthcare facilities
- Military bases and complexes
- Retail centers and outlets
- Schools and colleges

Other work environments have no walls. Take, for example, the forest ranger working for the US National Park Service. Although a portion of this role may be performed in an office environment, it can also be extremely mobile—moving from work setting to work setting in a car or truck—and then working in the outdoors most of the time.

Construction engineers, managers, and inspectors, as well as many of the skilled craftspeople (e.g., carpenters, welders, plumbers, electricians, etc.) who work in the building industry work in settings that are changing all the time. Their projects have a beginning, middle, and end and then they move on to the next setting and building project.

Information Contributes to Quality Decision Making

Career or occupational research is an essential part of the exploration process. It will move the explorer from a casual understanding of the career to a more detailed and formal view of the work and the people doing it. Along the path to career discovery, the explorer will learn things that resonate both positively and negatively. That's a sign that the information is teaching and helping. Good decisions require good research using the best information and resources available.

Frequently Asked Question

Question: Of the questions that young people have about future work, which are likely to produce answers that last over time?

Answer: The work that Americans do and the workplace where they do it are both subject to change. Many of the core tasks and responsibilities associated with specific occupations, however, will be the same in the future as they are today. Physicians are in the healing and illness prevention business. That is the constant. What changes is the "how" they heal or prevent. A new medicine could be under examination today and become available in six months that could dramatically impact the way physicians treat a particular illness or disease. Think of all career fields as having their constants but being affected in the ways the work is done and the way the workers perform.

Student Exercise 7.1

Career Research Outline: The Eleven Factor Method

Use the following eleven factors as the basic outline to conduct your research and create a profile of any career that holds interest for you. Take notes and develop profiles for comparative purposes as you refine your career options and make decisions about your future.

1. Nature and role definition
2. Settings where work is performed
3. Worker traits and characteristics
4. Locations where work will be found
5. Education and training required
6. Supply and demand
7. Potential to be influenced by change
8. Licenses, certifications, and other credentials
9. Compensation
10. Opportunities for growth, advancement, and mobility
11. Related careers and occupations

Student Exercise 7.2

Looking at Careers Using the Career Cluster Approach

One way career explorers can examine the future is by looking at the variety of occupations and careers that are performed in a particular field, setting, or cluster. In this exercise, each cluster will permit you to identify and consider the many occupations that are performed in the various settings. In each cluster you will identify careers and occupations that represent a mixture of educational requirements (e.g., specialized career training, college, etc.). Look at the short list of careers and occupations presented with each cluster in this chapter and then try to add five occupations to each cluster.

Advertising, Marketing, and Public Relations

_____

_____

Agriculture, Food, and Natural Resources

_____

_____

Architecture, Building, and Construction

_____

_____

Arts, Entertainment, and Humanities

_____

_____

Banking, Finance, and Investments

_____

_____

Business, Management, and Administration

_____

_____

Communications and Media

_____

_____

Environment

_____

_____

Government and Public Administration

_____

_____

Health and Medicine

_____

_____

Hospitality, Leisure, and Tourism

_____

_____

Human and Social Services

_____

_____

Information Technology

_____

_____

Law, Safety, Corrections, and Security

_____

_____

Manufacturing and Industry

_____

_____

Personal Services

_____

_____

Sales and Service

_____

_____

Science, Technology, Engineering, and Mathematics

_____

_____

Transportation, Distribution, and Logistics

_____

_____

Student Exercise 7.3

Comparing Career Strengths and Liabilities

In this chapter, you were encouraged to mount a more assertive search of careers and occupations and broaden your knowledge of the work, workers, and workplaces in the United States. In this exercise, you are asked to compare what you have learned about six careers or occupations that you have examined.

Career 1   Career 2   Career 3
Strengths: Things you liked about the career

_____   _____   _____

_____   _____   _____

Liabilities: Things you didn't like or would change about the career

_____   _____   _____

_____   _____   _____

Career 4   Career 5   Career 6
Strengths: Things you liked about the career

_____   _____   _____

_____   _____   _____

Liabilities: Things you didn't like or would change about the career

_____   _____   _____

_____   _____   _____

~

CHAPTER EIGHT

Sources of Information about Careers

I find that a great part of the information I have was acquired by looking up something and finding something else along the way.

—Franklin P. Adams, American journalist (1881–1960)

The world in which you live is a virtual career laboratory. Some careers are right in front of you—in school, in your community—everywhere you go. Others you get to see through television, the Internet, and the modern communication tools you use every day. Some—like the work of the oceanographer to a resident of Nebraska—will be a long distance from you but more recognizable when you get closer to them. Your sense of curiosity, coupled with your ability to investigate, will make the career laboratory in which you live come alive.

A number of reliable information sources have been used successfully to gain information that leads to greater career awareness. Regardless of your place in the career development process, any one or combination of the following sources can provide valuable information to help you prepare for future decisions.

Individuals currently working in specific careers can be a source of information to one examining that occupation or cluster of occupations. Informational interviews and opportunities to "shadow" people in their work settings are the best way to tap this resource. If people in a given career work in a variety of environments (e.g., nurses work in private practice, small clinic, and large hospital settings) they become familiar with as many different variations of the occupation as possible.

Should you have the opportunity to work part-time or during the summers, use those experiences to observe and study all of the people with whom you interface. Part-time and summer work may not be a precursor to the actual career you wish to pursue, but you can learn important lessons about teamwork, productivity, relationships, and other workplace values.

Career Literature

Guides, directories, and the larger career reference resources like the *Occupational Outlook Handbook* (comprehensive career directory) and the *Occupational Outlook Quarterly* (print and Internet magazine) of the US Department of Labor provide a wealth of information about many different careers. These publications can be found in many school and community libraries or by visiting the Labor Department website (www.dol.gov). These same libraries will also have guides and directories from other publishers. See the appendix for a list of some of the most popular career information publications.

Computer-Based Delivery Systems

Over the course of the past two decades many of the print resources used by students have been converted to computer or online delivery systems, including career and educational information databases. Similarly, many of the career interest and assessment instruments are now available in a computer styled delivery mechanism. School and college counselors and librarians are good resources as to where these contemporary delivery systems may be found.

Internet and Online Sources

There are so many places on the Internet where career explorers can find information to assist them in their personal career development that it would be futile to try to list them all here. The full *Occupational Outlook Handbook* of the US Department of Labor can be accessed at the https://www.bls.gov/ooh website.

Looking at specific occupations or careers will turn up a wealth of online information, including the possibility of participating in webinars and accessing podcasts. There are also a number of general self-help sites like www.myperfectresume.com where valuable information and links are available to the explorer. Ask your counselor what websites he or she recommends for someone who is at your particular place in the career development process.

In the appendix you will find a list of websites that provide a wealth of information and range of services for your career explorations.

Educational Programs and Institutions

Schools, colleges, and training programs provide information about careers they prepare people to enter. In addition, there will be many general school and college guides in your school or community library that present an array of educational options leading to career and work opportunities after graduation or completion of study requirements.

Major Employers

Companies, businesses, and firms, especially those employing large numbers of people in a specific career or career cluster (e.g., United Airlines for pilots, flight attendants, and airline personnel; Microsoft for computer analysts, programmers, and information technology specialists; and Ford for engineers and designers) provide both general information for career explorers and specific employment information for job seekers.

Many large firms have a "Careers" link on their website. Accessing the *Fortune* magazine annual list of the largest businesses (known as the Fortune 500) will link the career explorer to the largest US and global employers.

Organizations of Professional and Skilled Workers

Professional and trade associations, representing people in a specific career, field, or industry, have been first-rate sources of both occupational and educational information for many years. Organizations like the National League of Nursing (nursing careers), National Association of Broadcasters (television and radio careers), American Chemical Society (chemist and science careers), and many similar groups create and disseminate literature and media about careers in their areas of special interest. In the appendix, you will find a list, including general website addresses, of professional and trade organizations that produce educational and career information.

The *Encyclopedia of Associations* and *Directory of National Trade and Professional Associations* are excellent references to these groups, and one or both reference guides are likely to be found in your community library. Students can acquire the career and education resources of these organizations by sending them a letter or postcard or contacting them via their website. Each organization distributes career and educational information as a public service and most of the time it is free.

Government Agencies

The largest employer of people in the United States is the federal government. Add state and local government to the federal work numbers and you have a significant number of people and positions. Because the government employs such a large number of people, federal, state, and local agencies have generated career information resources describing the positions available and the qualifications they seek in candidates. One of the easiest ways to learn of these careers is to conduct an Internet search using "Careers in the Department of [insert name of agency]" in a popular Internet search engine like www.google.com, www.ask.com, or www.yahoo.com.

The branches of the US military represent an incredible number of opportunities for both educational and career experiences. Explorers can learn about the opportunities available for both officers and enlisted personnel in each branch of military service by contacting the following websites:

- Air Force—http://www.airforce.com
- Army—http://goarmy.com
- Coast Guard—http://www.gocoastguard.com
- Marine Corps—http://www.marines.com
- Navy—http://www.navy.com

Finally, the federal government via the US Department of Labor (www.dol.gov), as well as affiliated state agencies, has a vast number of resources and links that will aid explorers in learning about opportunities and making quality decisions.

Making Certain the Information You Are Using Is the Best

Individuals who are serious about studying a variety of career options will find an array of information tools and resources at their disposal, and care must be taken to make certain the information being used is the best available. Applying the following evaluation points will ensure the information is of the highest quality:

- **Source:** Who is the creator and disseminator of the information and what is their motivation for making it available? The vast majority of career and education information sources are reputable and reliable, but one must be vigilant in checking both the content and the motivation of the source. Many information creators see this work as a public service. It is their way of ensuring that consumers have an accurate and current depiction of the work performed in their career or field.

Be wary of print and electronic messages offering "guaranteed entry" or "unlimited opportunity."

- **Accuracy:** Does the information depict the occupation or career in a comprehensive and correct manner? Many careers combine both positive (e.g., opportunity to travel) and not so positive aspects (e.g., reporters for the Weather Channel report often from the midst of hurricanes, tornadoes, and other dangerous weather situations). Does the information present opposing or contradictory views in a candid, realistic manner?
- **Age:** When was the information created? A piece of information that is five years old is considered an antique to most. Parts of some career information do not change with time, but others, like employment outlook data, can change dramatically in just a short period of time.
- **Number sensitivity:** Nothing will make a piece of career or educational information more inaccurate more quickly than a number. Information like the cost of tuition, hours required for certification, and other similar data needs to be "second-sourced" to ensure their accuracy.
- **Free of bias:** Does the producer and disseminator of the information have any particular reason to shade the truth or distort the facts? Many for-profit career schools, for example, use their career information to recruit students and have been known to go overboard in presenting only a positive picture. If something appears "too good to be true," it is probably worth checking.
- **Utility:** What some will suggest is career and education information may be laden with statistics and terminology that make it far from "user friendly." Attempt to use information whose creator had the career explorer in mind when the information was generated, and it will be more likely to pass the utility test.

All career and educational information needs to be examined to ensure accuracy, relevance, and utility. When you question or doubt anything, including the information presented by people (human resources), don't fail to validate the information by using an alternative source.

Information Is Everywhere!

Career information surrounds you. What was once difficult to find and often suspect due to age and accuracy is today abundant and of much better quality. Make the world of work your classroom and access all the information that valuable and trusted sources of information make available to you.

Don't underestimate the value that hands-on information experiences can have in allowing you to interface with people in varying occupations and experience settings (e.g., hospitals, retail establishments, school, etc.) where much of the work in the United States is performed. Such experiences will pay huge personal dividends.

Knowing as much as you can will help you decide if a particular occupation is something you will want to do in the future—one that will begin as an occupation and, with time and experience, grow to become your life's work, your career.

Career Fact: Statistics Are Important in Examining the Present and Future of Any Career

Many of the questions an explorer will have about a specific career or the world of work in general can be answered by the statistics derived from personal research. It is important, however, to look to experienced providers and reliable sources (e.g., Bureau of Labor Statistics [BLS], US Department of Labor) for this information. Statistics are great at projecting demand and providing descriptive information such as how much one can expect to earn in a particular occupation. For earnings and employment information by occupation, industry, and geographic area, checks the BLS Occupational Employment Statistics survey, online at https://www.census.gov/programs-surveys/cps.html.

Several other good statistics sources include:

- National Compensation Survey—Information about wages and earnings. Online at www.bls.gov/ncs
- Current Population Survey—Information about educational attainment, self-employment, and work hours. Online at https://www.census.gov/programs-surveys/cps.html
- National Association of Colleges and Employers—Data on entry-level information for college graduates by major and industry. Online at www.naceweb.org

Frequently Asked Questions

Question: Of all the information used to describe careers and occupations, what is the most volatile in terms of staying current and accurate?

Answer: There are many things that can affect the life of an otherwise good piece of career information, but explorers need to be particularly sensitive to numbers and statistics. Employment trend projections at the beginning of the current millennium caught most analysts off guard because they did not predict the impact the 2008 recession and economic downturn would have on the economy. Unemployment rates in the United States eventually exceeded 10 percent of the population and affected millions of people, an impact that was second only to the Great Depression eighty years previous. Other numbers like tuition costs and study time requirements are frequently changing and should be validated before decisions are made that use such information.

Question: What are the benefits of part-time, summer, and volunteer work in helping one to learn about the workplace?

Answer: When a career explorer accepts any kind of paid or volunteer work experience or becomes part of an internship or work-study program in their education, he or she is assuming the responsibilities associated with that position. Each experience teaches the importance of accepting and completing assignments, appearing on time, contributing a quality effort, and becoming part of a team that is responsible for delivering a product or service. These are the same tasks that will be associated with your first "real" job and all that will eventually follow and constitute your career. In addition, the positions that put money in your purse or wallet also will teach lessons about money management, budgeting, and saving.

Question: Are people working in a given career considered a fairly reliable source of information about the occupation?

Answer: People performing an occupational role, for the most part, can be considered accurate and reliable sources of information. Each is performing the tasks and experiencing a level of success and satisfaction. The lessons you learn from occupational occupants can usually be as real and current as you can find anywhere.

There will be, however, the occasional exception—the individual who hasn't stayed on top of his or her profession and may not be representative of where the occupation is currently or where it is going. This is clearly an instance when any information accuracy doubts generated by a human resource should be checked with a second source or presented to a counselor for examination.

Student Exercise 8.1

Using Career Resources

In the space provided, keep track of the various publications, Internet sites, podcasts, DVDs, video programs, and related career guidance resources that you use in career exploration. Be certain to identify where you found the resource (e.g., library, career center, college center, etc.) in case you wish to use it later in the process. An example is provided

Resource Title	Location	Comments
Occupational Outlook Handbook	Library	Great overview of many occupations
_____	_____	_____
_____	_____	_____
_____	_____	_____
_____	_____	_____

Student Exercise 8.2

Considering Career Options and Making Tentative Decisions

List five careers (in any order) for which you would like to give additional consideration and attention at this time. To the right, offer an appraisal as to whether the career as you currently know it is an "excellent" or "good" fit for you or one to which you want to devote more study. Then insert up to five reasons to support your assessment.

Your counselor can help you with this appraisal. As you prepare this list, concentrate on the career attributes that appeal to you and record them. Chances are likely your future career—whether one of these five—will possess similar attributes.

Career _____ Excellent _____ Good _____ More study _____

1. _____
2. _____
3. _____
4. _____
5. _____

Career _____ Excellent _____ Good _____ More study _____

1. _____
2. _____
3. _____
4. _____
5. _____

Career _____ Excellent _____ Good _____ More study _____

1. _____
2. _____

3. _____

4. _____

5. _____

Career _____ Excellent _____ Good _____ More study _____

1. _____

2. _____

3. _____

4. _____

5. _____

Career _____ Excellent _____ Good _____ More study _____

1. _____

2. _____

3. _____

4. _____

5. _____

Career _____ Excellent _____ Good _____ More study _____

1. _____

2. _____

3. _____

4. _____

5. _____

CHAPTER NINE

~

Relating Education to Career Development

It's what you learn after you know it all that counts.

—John Wooden, UCLA Hall of Fame
basketball coach and ten-time NCAA national champion

The influence of education and training in your career cannot be understated. Education prepares you. It then leads you through the career development process and influences your success and mobility. Although many different factors will be influential in your future, none will be greater than education and training, a constant in your life for as long as you work. Education will open doors and light paths from now until the day you elect not to work any longer.

Your success in the high school or college classroom—as measured by your grades and the comfort you feel studying a particular subject—can be an indicator that you will enjoy a career that depends on and uses that body of knowledge and the skills that will emerge from learning. There will even be instances like in law, engineering, nursing, and accounting when you will be required to study a standard curriculum and pass an examination to become certified or achieve the required credentials to practice that profession. Similar tests of one's knowledge and skill will be required before one can practice skilled occupations such as electrician, plumber, and machinist.

Your early studies are important for several reasons. First, you develop your academic skills for later education. Second, you develop a learner profile in high school and college that will be with you for life. The study skills you acquire and the manner you approach your academic work are likely to set the tone for the way you approach education and learning for the rest of your life. Finally, the things you study and their application in the world of work will become valuable lessons for you.

Relating What You Study to Future Careers

Each of the major subjects that you study—English, foreign language, mathematics, science, and social studies—has relevance to the workplace. Knowledge you acquire in these subjects can be applied in a variety of work environments and used over and over again. Skills you master, like problem solving and computation, are tools that workers need in every part of the US workplace. Students who achieve and enjoy a particular area of study should examine careers that call on comparable knowledge and skill.

Consider the relationship that the various school subjects have for careers by examining each.

English

Have you enjoyed success in your English and literature classes? Do you have good communications (oral and written) skills? Language skills are important to these careers:

- Actor/actress
- Advertising/promotion manager
- Business manager
- Court reporter
- Editor
- Historian
- Interpreter
- Journalist/reporter
- Lawyer
- Librarian
- Marketing director
- Media producer
- Public relations specialist
- Salesperson
- Speech/language pathologist
- Teacher/professor
- Website designer
- Writer

Foreign Language
Do you like a particular language? Have you become fluent in a second or third language? Language proficiency can be useful in the following careers:

- Broadcaster
- Buyer
- Customer service representative
- Economist
- English as a second language (ESL) educator
- Flight attendant
- Foreign service officer
- International trade analyst
- Interpreter
- Librarian
- Pilot
- Teacher/professor
- Teacher aide (bilingual)
- Tour director/guide
- Translator

Mathematics
Have you done well in algebra, geometry, and calculus? Do you have good reasoning and computational skills? These careers rely heavily on a solid knowledge of mathematical concepts:

- Accountant/auditor
- Actuary
- Architect
- Carpenter
- Computer engineer
- Demographer
- Draftsman
- Engineer
- Industrial engineer
- Investment advisor
- Machinist
- Mechanic
- Meteorologist
- Research scientist
- Software engineer

- Statistician
- Surveyor
- Systems analyst

Science

Do you like science? Have you achieved good grades in biology, chemistry, and physics? Do you like to experiment and study technical subjects? Do you have an inquisitive mind? If yes, you may want to consider the following careers:

- Astronaut
- Astronomer
- Biologist
- Botanist
- Chemist
- Environmental engineer
- Geophysicist
- Instrument designer
- Laboratory technician
- Oceanographer
- Pharmacist
- Physician
- Physicist
- Research engineer
- Solar engineer
- Technical writer
- Veterinarian
- Zoologist

Social Studies

Have history, government, and social studies been your favorite subjects? Do you enjoy dealing with people issues and problems? If yes, you may find success in the following careers:

- Anthropologist
- Business administrator
- Community agency director
- Consumer advocate
- Counselor
- Curator

- Educator
- Entrepreneur/business owner
- Human resource director
- Lawyer
- Minister/rabbi/priest
- Museum educator
- Police officer
- Psychologist
- Recreation program director
- Sociologist

Note: Do not consider these lists complete or exhaustive. Each represents a sampling of the careers and occupations that can be linked to achievement and success in each of the study areas. Student Exercise 9.1 will engage you in a more intensive examination of the relationship of school studies to careers.

Career Fact: More than Four Thousand US Institutions Offer Degree-Granting Postsecondary Education Opportunities in the United States
The US higher education enterprise is the finest in the world. In addition to more than four thousand degree-granting (i.e., associate, baccalaureate, graduate, first-professional) institutions, there are countless other educational opportunities to study in certificate and apprenticeship programs—not to mention the number of educational paths offered by employers and the military. Education for career opportunity abounds in the United States.

Frequently Asked Question
    Question: I find all subjects in school to be challenging. How can I relate my future career interests to subjects that don't come naturally to me?
    Answer: Remember what was stated about innate abilities and aptitudes. Some people are better at learning than others. Things like reading, problem solving, research, and writing may not be as difficult for them as they are for you. Different people may take different routes and end up at the same place.

        For you, the academic challenges in some subject areas may be more formidable, but you have still discovered a way to achieve good or reasonable grades. Possibly it was more time or attention or you simply had to work a little harder. The fact that you succeeded is all that matters. And while you may elect a career in an area that is naturally more comfortable or one where you seem to excel with minimum effort, your successes in more difficult studies allow you to keep careers related to them under extended consideration.

Choosing a career is not about electing to go down the path of least resistance—the easiest educational route. Subjects that you study in the school or college classroom, however, can be indicators of the application of knowledge in career and occupational circumstances. Listen to what those indicators tell you.

Student Exercise 9.1

Relating Careers to Study

Consider the body of knowledge you study and the skills that you master in each of the areas listed and add five occupations where that learning could be put to good use in the workplace. Focus on careers and occupations that hold particular appeal to you.

English   Science   Foreign Language

_____   _____   _____

_____   _____   _____

_____   _____   _____

_____   _____   _____

_____   _____   _____

Social Studies   Mathematics   Computer/Information Study

_____   _____   _____

_____   _____   _____

_____   _____   _____

_____   _____   _____

~

CHAPTER TEN

Educational Paths to Careers

Let us think of education as the means of developing our greatest abilities, because in each of us there is a private hope and dream which, fulfilled, can be translated into benefit for everyone and greater strength for our nation.

—John F. Kennedy, thirty-fifth president of the United States

Education will play an important role in your preparation for and mobility within your career. You started down the path toward your career the day you started preschool or kindergarten. All learning becomes the foundation for the knowledge and skills you will use in the workplace.

As you think about the work roles you wish to assume one day, you also need to consider the educational path you will need to follow to ensure successful entry and transition into that career. Some of those paths are immediately before you—ones you are looking at right now as opportunities and options are being studied. Others are off in the distance and will play a significant part of your career development for a long time.

Educational Paths Immediately before You
The educational paths likely to be in your immediate future include the following:

College and University Study. According to the Digest of Education Statistics of the US Department of Education, the United States is home to 710 public and 2,296 four-year institutions today. Include for-profit and online degree-granting institutions and the total number of four-year colleges exceeds 3,500. These colleges offer baccalaureate (e.g., Bachelor of Science, Bachelor of Arts, etc.) degrees in a wide array of majors or fields of study.

Liberal arts study includes such areas as history, philosophy, language, and literature that, although not tied to a particular career, will prepare the student with a well-rounded education that is valued and desired by many employers. Other college studies (e.g., business, communications, engineering, education, etc.) are more focused and allow degree earners to ease directly into corresponding careers. A growing number of colleges and universities offer extended learning experiences that combine study in the classroom with an internship or practical experiences in business, industry, or related work settings. College degrees are required for entry into most professional careers.

The majority of four-year colleges are residential, thus offering students the experience of living and learning in the same environment. Students can begin their postsecondary education at the community/junior college level and then transfer to a four-year institution.

Community, Junior, and Technical College study. Education programs that prepare students for both career entry and continued study at a four-year college. Most two-year community colleges are nonresidential, although some junior colleges do provide housing and living services. Short-term and one-year programs generally lead to certificates, although full study in two-year programs typically result in earning the Associate of Arts degree. The Digest of Education Statistics indicates there were 1,579 two-year degree-granting institutions in the United States in 2017.

Specialized Career, Technical, and Vocational Study. Short- or limited-term, focused training leading to direct entry into the workforce. Graduates achieve certificates or diplomas and typically meet entry requirements for specific occupations. This form of study can be initiated either at the secondary school level or in postsecondary education. Career, technical, and vocational study is offered in secondary schools, postsecondary institutions, and at more than 15,000 focused or specialized (e.g., culinary studies, graphic design, heavy equipment operation, etc.) institutions offering career training. A significant number of these institutions are for-profit in their business structure.

Apprenticeship or Industry Sponsored Training. Hands-on experiential learning in one of many skilled craft or trade areas. Apprenticeship programs, often sponsored by industry and union organizations, are designed to meet entry standards for a particular occupation. Individuals completing an apprenticeship program typically transition directly from training to their occupation.

Employer and Industry Sponsored Training. Educational experiences provided by or supported by firms, businesses, and organizations wishing to maximize the ongoing knowledge acquisition and skill set development of their workforce. Sometimes referred to as on-the-job training or OJT, these training programs typically focus on a specific curriculum that will improve and extend employee productivity and performance.

Military Education and Training. Broad offering of career training opportunities related to the needs of the armed services. The branches of the US military afford career aspirants a number of educational venues to pursue hundreds of occupational interests while serving in the defense of the nation. Experiences in the Air Force, Army, Coast Guard, Marine Corps, and Navy can also help the service member prepare for and pay for postsecondary education experiences after enlistment.

Educational Paths off in the Distance

After you have moved through the kindergarten to college experience, possibly after you have entered and been active in the working world, other educational paths will come into view and play a role in your career development.

Graduate and professional school. Study beyond the undergraduate level leading to a master's degree, doctorate, or first-professional degree.

Some students will continue on to such programs immediately following college, and others will opt to get some work experience under their belt before pursuing these advanced studies. At this level, the competition for admission is intense and the academic requirements are stringent. Many graduate students mix career and study.

Lifelong or continuing education. Student engagement in either independent or employer-supported training that is career or occupationally oriented. Increasingly, career mobility and advancement will be tied to the individual's ability to keep learning and growing in their area of work expertise. In some instances that will involve returning to an academic environment to earn the next degree or participate in seminars or workshops.

In others, the educational experience (i.e., certificate programs acknowledging advanced study, employer led in-service education, etc.) will be provided internally in the work environment as a part of employee professional development programs and in-service education. Finally, distance learning and online educational experiences, along with personal reading and research, will become vehicles workers will use to continue their career education.

Getting Answers to Education Questions

During the exploration process students will have an opportunity to ask a lot of questions to find the institutions and programs that meet the academic, environmental, and financial requirements that they have established as important. The decision whether to apply to a college, for example, may be tied directly to the information that is collected and the impressions that are made during this evaluative process.

Following are a number of questions that you, the student, should ask as part of this exploration. The list should not be viewed as exhaustive (you will certainly think of others), and they are not presented in any kind of priority order.

Program of study/academic philosophy/reputation. Does the college offer the academic specialty you wish to pursue? What is the academic reputation of the institution in general and the program (e.g., journalism, engineering, etc.) in particular? Do graduates get good jobs, and are they admitted to grad school? Does the college have a strong library and use the latest tools and technology to educate its students? What are the requirements for success in the classroom? Does the institution ascribe to a particular philosophy of teaching or learning? What is the typical class size? Do the best professors teach classes at the undergraduate level?

Admission requirements and competition. How will your abilities, aptitudes, and previous achievements stack up against those of other applicants and enrolled students? How have students with your academic credentials fared in the admission process? What is the profile of the typical student at the college? What percentage of admitted students graduate? How many years does it take a typical student to earn a degree?

Location/setting. Are you interested in going to a college nearby, in the state or region, or anywhere in the United States or the world? Do you have a preference for the type of community (e.g., large city, small city, rural) where the college is located? How important is the campus setting (e.g., open spaces and tree-filled lawns or high-rise buildings)?

Institutional characteristics. What type of institution best suits your academic and environmental needs? Do you prefer a large university with multiple academic venues, a small liberal arts college, or something in between? Do you want to study at a two- or four-year college? Do you prefer a public or private, coeducational or single-sex, church-affiliated or career-oriented institution?

Accommodations. Are the dormitories comfortable and well furnished? Will the food service respond to your dietary needs? Can your physical fitness and recreational interests be satisfied? Is living on campus mandatory? What percentage of students live off campus?

Social, cultural, and extracurricular atmospheres. What social, cultural, and leisure time opportunities are available? Do you have interests outside of the classroom (e.g., music, sports, drama, or volunteerism) that you would like to maintain while in college? If so, will the college or the community allow you to pursue those interests? Is there a church, synagogue, mosque, or other related congregation on campus or in the community that will satisfy your faith-based interests?

Special needs and considerations. Can the college respond to tutorial, counseling, health, or other special needs that you might have? Does the institution offer a varied menu of social and cultural experiences beyond the classroom? Does the campus and surrounding community present a secure living environment?

Cost. What is the cost of tuition, room and board, and fees? What personal (e.g., transportation) costs will be required? What financial aid opportunities exist, and what are the qualifications? Is financial need factored into the admission decision? Are there opportunities for part-time work on campus or in the community?

It will be next to impossible to find any college that gets a five-star rating in each of these areas of exploration. In the final analysis, does the college or postsecondary education experience present you with a good feeling? Is it a place where you see yourself learning and living over the next four or more years? If the answer is yes, the next step is to get an application for admission.

Determining the Best Educational Option

Somewhere in the vast network of more than four thousand US two- and four-year colleges, there are a number that are right for the prospective applicant. As students refine and narrow that list, their evaluative filter should focus on these issues:

Academic fit. Is the college the right place for a particular student to learn? Does it offer courses and curriculum that are consistent with the student's educational and career objectives? Will the student be challenged academically and be capable of meeting all challenges?

Environmental fit. Is the college the right place for a particular student to live? The college-bound student is about to become a citizen of a college or university for the next four years or more, and he or she needs to feel comfortable, safe, and content in the collegiate setting (campus and beyond).

Affordability. What are the costs of enrollment, room and board, fees and such, and what kind of financial aid is available? In the current economy, students and their parents are becoming more budget and cost conscious, and steps needs to be taken to find the most affordable institutions.

Admissibility. A final aspect of college exploration is to look at the profiles of admitted students to see if those characteristics and traits are consistent with those that will be presented by the applicant. College expectations of students can vary from year to year, and knowing this information in advance might be a critical factor in the inclusion of an institution on the application list or going through the throes of making an application. Ask any college under consideration for a copy of its most recent freshman class profile, the document that contains the information you wish to review.

Note: Although the information just presented has focused on the school-to-college transition, students considering career or vocational training programs must use similar criteria in determining the suitability and fit of programs and experiences they are considering.

Education: An Essential Ingredient in Your Future

Futurists point to the current and continuing explosion of new knowledge as a matter all future workers must address. Knowledge and tools that you take for granted today didn't exist in the early work world of your parents. Similarly, knowledge and skills they brought to their early careers have been replaced by new information and more contemporary methods and tools. Things that are considered commonplace today (e.g., the Internet, cell phones, facsimile machines, etc.) all emerged in a thirty-year period in the latter part of the last century.

Education is the only way that individuals can be assured that they possess what they need to know to keep them at a high level of career capability and competence. The bottom line is that learning never ceases. Change is the only constant, and ongoing learning and continuing education are the only mechanisms the worker has to resist becoming obsolete and, even worse, unemployed.

Education Plus Experience

There are a number of careers for which one cannot formally prepare in a classroom. The study of the law can prepare one to be a practicing lawyer or possibly teach in a law school, but to become a judge, the professional lawyer usually needs to have a record of career experiences that prepare him or her to be elected or appointed to a judgeship. The same is true of career positions like astronaut and editor. A review of NASA astronaut profiles will point out that they generally come from varied backgrounds as military officers, pilots, engineers, and scientists. Editors most likely have had experience as journalists or writers before assuming any editing duties.

Tangible Benefits of Learning

Information collected and reported by the US Census Bureau has documented a consistent increase in the educational attainment of the population since the data was first collected in the middle of the last century. Among younger adults (ages 25–29) in 2008, 88 percent had completed high school and 31 percent had completed college.

There is corresponding data to show that each level of educational attainment corresponds to greater earning power for the employee. Finally, the greater one's educational attainment, the less likely he or she will be affected by job loss or layoff when there is an economic downturn. These are certainly factors the career explorers may need to build into their decision-making formula.

The Importance of Certification, Licensure, and Credentialing

There are a host of careers and occupations for which one must earn and maintain a credential advanced by their profession and monitored by certification organizations or state agencies. The credentials of professional organizations are often referred to as *certification*, and those administered by state agencies are called *licenses*. Licensure requirements for an occupation (e.g., counselor, dental hygienist, lawyer, realtor, etc.) often vary from state to state. Individuals not holding these credentials are not permitted to perform these occupations.

Certification and licensing have multiple purposes. First, it is an indicator that the certificate holder or licensee has met a certain educational or performance standard and earned the credential. Certification is typically a national standard managed by a professional organization or trade society.

One such example is the Certified Public Accountant (CPA) credential of the American Institute of Certified Public Accountants.

Others would be the National Certified Counselor (NCC) certificate conferred by the National Board of Certified Counselors (NBCC) and Certificates of Clinical Competence (CCC-A and CCC-SLP) awarded to audiologists and speech-language pathologists, respectively, by the American Speech-Language and Hearing Association. Often these societies also oversee the accreditation of education and training programs leading up to the individual's application for certification.

Certification and licensure have yet another purpose in that they tell the consuming public that the accountant or audiologist or mechanic they are dealing with has earned the appropriate professional or trade credential, a sign not necessarily of specific expertise but rather that he or she is a bona fide professional or craftsperson and has met the standards deemed necessary to practice that occupation. Individuals who become certified and licensed are usually required to engage in and complete specified levels of continuing education to maintain their credential.

Career Fact: The More You Learn, the More You Earn

One of the realities of the US workplace is that the more you learn, the more you earn. Another fact is that the higher your educational attainment level, the less likely it will be that you will find yourself unemployed or underemployed. According to the US Census Bureau and the US Department of Labor, the median household income level for a high school diploma was $44,970 compared with those with a bachelor's degree which was $91,772. As the educational attainment level increases, so do earnings.

Career Myth: Career Opportunities Are Restricted to Educational and Training Achievements and Levels

You will certainly see many vacant positions that call for study in a particular area (e.g., accounting, education, engineering, etc.) or a credential in a given field (e.g., registered nurse, licensed psychologist, etc.). Similarly, many employers will indicate their preference for college graduates or some other level of educational attainment. What may surprise you, however, is the willingness of a growing number of employers to accept personal characteristics, accomplishments, and practical experience in lieu of formal education, specific study, or training.

The computer industry is an excellent example. Many people currently working in computer and information technology studied other things first and eventually gravitated to the computer applications in those fields. Another consideration is that many skills, once learned, can be applied in a multitude of settings and environments. Finally, college graduates with degrees in liberal arts are working in every field imaginable. Their study focus did not impose any limitations.

Career Myth: Elite Colleges Produce the Most Successful Leaders in the United States

Ivy League universities, the service academies, and prestigious colleges of both a public and private nature have an outstanding record of producing leaders for business, government, military, and other sectors. The United States has had presidents from Columbia University (Barack Obama), Yale University (George W. Bush and George H. W. Bush), Georgetown University (Bill Clinton), and the US Naval Academy (Jimmy Carter) but also from Eureka College (Ronald Reagan), Whittier College (Richard Nixon), and Southwest Texas State Teachers College (now University of Texas–San Marcos; Lyndon Johnson). Colin Powell, former US Secretary of State, army general, and chairman of the Joint Chiefs of Staff, is a graduate of the City College of New York. Entertainer and businesswoman Oprah Winfrey earned her degree at Tennessee State University.

Similarly, Fortune 500 CEOs have hailed from a variety of institutions like Pittsburg State University (Kansas), University of Texas, Gannon University, Georgia State University, and Central Oklahoma University. A number of "high achievers" in their respective fields didn't complete their college experience, including Microsoft founder Bill Gates (Harvard University) and CNN founder Ted Turner (Brown University). US leaders in business, military, government, and other domains represent many different educational levels and institutions, many of which wouldn't make the "elite" category, should there be an accurate definition of that term. What they do have in common are character traits—vision, tenacity, inventiveness, effectiveness, and commitment—that exceed those of their counterparts.

Frequently Asked Questions

Question: Will there ever be a time when I won't have to learn anymore?

Answer: There was a time when an individual could acquire the knowledge and skills needed to last a long time in her or his chosen occupation. This is not the case any longer. The knowledge explosion in every field of endeavor, coupled with the emergence of new and innovative tools of the workplace, dictate the critical need for ongoing study and learning. This is clearly one of those places where the "you snooze, you lose" adage is applicable.

Question: When a license or certification is associated with a career, does it mean that people who do not hold that credential are prohibited from performing that occupational role?

Answer: Yes. Licenses and certificates are awarded by state agencies and professional organizations, respectively, as a means of protecting the public and ensuring that certain standards have been met by the person performing a particular occupation. Savvy consumers look for these credentials. In the case of state licensure laws, people who have not met these requirements are prohibited from practicing these professions and occupations.

Student Exercise 10.1

Educational Paths to Career Entry

As your career exploration reveals schools, colleges, and other learning venues that will prepare you for entry into the field or fields that interest you, keep a running log of those institutions and preparation programs. If you have identified a website, publication, or other resource that will explain the preparation program in greater detail, make note of it in your log. An example is provided for you.

Career/occupation   School, college, training program, etc.

Graphic artist   Independence Community College, Freedom, PA

www.independencecc.edu

_____

_____

_____

_____

_____

_____

_____

CHAPTER ELEVEN

~

Identifying Job Opportunities

Find a job you like and you add five days to every week.

—H. Jackson Brown, Jr. author of *Life's Little Instruction Book*

Mounting an effective job search is, in many ways, exploration all over again. Only now you possess career knowledge and skill set, and the challenge is to convince an employer that you are capable of performing an occupational role. The searches that you conduct as a student, whether in high school or college, will become learning experiences. How you identify employment opportunities and the steps you take to get hired will be experiences that stay with you for life, and you can call upon them every time you seek to enter or move about the world of work.

Designing and Implementing a Job-Seeking Campaign
Finding a job is work—hard work. The first phase of the search is all about identifying employers, both those that offer occupational or job opportunities in your field of work and those that have current vacancies. Knowing the identities of employers that may offer you employment should begin at some time during knowledge and skill acquisition. Beginning this early will allow you to track trends and opportunities and be ready to mount your personal search more effectively.

As you close out this part of your education and begin to test the employment waters, the process will intensify and just knowing where you might work will become who has active vacancies for the work that you are qualified to perform and is ready to hire. This chapter addresses the job identification strategies, and chapter 12 delves into the specific communication tools that the active job seeker must create at different times. Chapter 13 then addresses the approaches that will lead to successful interviews.

Vehicles of Learning of Employment Opportunities

Suggestions have been offered regarding how to examine careers and determine if there is a particular fit between you and the occupation. The same strategies should be used to look for employment and make the transition to the workplace. You can also sharpen these job-seeking skills when you apply for summer and part-time employment as a student.

Employment Postings

Newspapers have been a source of job postings since the early days of publishing. Employers who want to make their vacancy known to a large pool of prospective applicants often use the employment pages in the classified section of their community newspaper.

Employment positions are also posted with state and local community agencies that help unemployed and underemployed individuals as a part of their mission. Most of these agencies function as services of state and local government, and many are tied together as a national network by the US Department of Labor. Services are also provided by the career planning and placement offices at many schools and colleges.

Internet, Social Media, and Electronic Job Boards

The Internet has, in many respects, replaced the newspaper as the universal "connector" of people to jobs. People shop on the Internet. They go to school on the Internet. Why not use the Internet then to look for a job and communicate with individuals who may have job information to share with you?

General Assistance

There are so many places on the Internet where career explorers can find information to assist them in their personal career development that it would be futile to try to list them all here. Looking at specific occupations or careers will turn up a wealth of online information. There are also a number of general self-help sites offered by the US Department of Labor, state departments of labor, and other organizations.

Many of the print sources mentioned previously also offer their career stories via online blogs and exchanges. Ask a counselor what websites he or she recommends for someone who is at your particular place in the career development process. In the appendix you will find a list of websites offering a wealth of information

The Riley Guide was created by a former university librarian, Margaret E. Diker, to help job seekers find employment, and it has become one of the most popular websites on the Internet. At www.myperfectresume.com job seekers will find a wealth of general information about the career development process and link after link to job search resources. Two other Internet sites worth using are www.CareerOneStop.org and www.job-hunt.org.

Social Media Sites

Social media sites like Facebook, Twitter, Instagram, Pinterest, LinkedIn, or others have become a popular vehicle for how Americans learn what is happening in the world and how they communicate with others. A recent survey by the Pew Research Center Internet and American Life Project discovered that eight in ten Internet-using Americans were subscribers to Facebook or some other form of social media. With that level of exposure, it is little wonder this burgeoning medium is being used to identify jobs and communicate the availability of prospective employees.

Social media use is also used by employers. A recent CareerBuilder.com posting conveyed that 37 percent of employers surveyed used social networks to screen candidates. How influential those findings are in determining how many job offers are being made may be impossible to determine, but the greater the use is, the greater the influence potential. When queried by CareerBuilder as to the motivation of screening candidates via social media, the responses ranged from wanting to see the person in their lifestyle and work culture to a desire to learn more about work experiences and qualifications to the frank response of looking for reasons "not to hire."

Job Boards

Once you are ready for job entry, a number of developing job boards, which are often established around business and occupational schemes, represent sound gateways for job identification and application. The Pew Research Center found recently that 40 percent of all library Internet users went online to look for a job or use or access other employment information.

The global technology you use today has had a two-edged impact on the job search process. From your desk, or anywhere for that matter, the Internet allows you to search for jobs anywhere in the United States or the world.

Online visitors can sort opportunities by occupation, cluster, employer, setting, location, and any number of other classifications. That's the good news. The bad news is you have to sort through the glut of listings to identify those which are relevant to your specific search. It sounds hard to believe, but in some occupations in some industries, the overload of information can be bewildering.

Electronic job boards come in several varieties. First you have large, national boards representing every occupation under the sun. There are also a large number of niche boards that focus on jobs in a particular occupational area (i.e., sales and marketing, information technology, etc.), level (i.e., executive, manager, supervisor, etc.), setting (i.e., government, health care, etc.), or location. Job boards also have a feature that allows job seekers to post their résumé electronically, thus permitting employers to conduct searches that may result in personal contact with the job seeker. These services then encourage the contacted party to submit an e-mail letter if they are interested in applying for the position.

A number of the more popular Internet job boards are identified in the appendix.

Professional and Trade Associations

Many professional and trade associations support their own job boards and provide services to their members using the Internet, publications, and offering face-to-face services at their annual meetings. The American Counseling Association (ACA), for example, aids members in finding counseling positions through Internet postings, employment opportunity ads in *Counseling Today* magazine, and a face-to-face (employer and applicant) activity at the ACA annual conference. Association membership is also considered a valuable networking opportunity that often leads to the sharing of information about industry vacancies.

Business and Corporate Websites

A search of websites of businesses, firms, and corporations that employ persons from a particular cluster of occupations is likely to turn up an "Employment" link or "Jobs" links. Human resources officers use these links to post everything from vacant full-time positions to temporary positions and internship possibilities. Visitors will find everything from the position descriptions to the procedures, often online, that interested individuals should follow to apply.

For example, a nurse interested in working in Atlanta, Georgia, would find valuable information by visiting EmoryHealthcare.com, a unit with ties to Emory University Hospital. The job seeker will find EmoryHealthcare. com is connected to nine clinics, hospitals, partners, and related healthcare providers, each representing nursing and other job opportunities.

Search and Staffing Firms

Search and staffing firms have set as their mission the placement of individuals in employment situations that will help them satisfy their career aspirations and employment circumstances that will help the individual achieve personal satisfaction at that particular point in their career development. This can be at career entry or at times when growth and mobility have arisen.

These firms support the work performed by human resources officers in corporations, businesses, organizations, and agencies as they seek to fill vacancies established by the employer. Upon registration with the search and staffing firm, the candidate for employment will be made aware of relevant postings and guided in the remainder of the search and selection process by a staff member. Users of search and staffing services should enlist professionals who hold the Certified Personnel Consultant (CPC) certificate of the National Association of Personnel Services (NAPS).

Career Planning and Placement Centers

Most institutions of learning offer students transitioning into the workplace the opportunity to use the services of their counselors and placement officers as they transition from these educational settings to full-time employment. Services such as hosting employers with vacancies, job boards, mock interviews, and job search workshops are among those typically offered in these settings.

These programs and their services are likely to abide by the comprehensive standards and practices created by the National Career Development Association (NCDA), the National Association of Colleges and Employers (NACE), and the National Association of Student Personnel Administrators (NASPA).

Networking

"It's not what you know, but who you know" is a view that is often voiced by frustrated job seekers, suggesting that good jobs are often hidden from public view. If true, the networks that a job seeker constructs or participates in can be a strong source of information about new or vacant positions, changing workplace conditions, and other factors that typically result in exposure to opportunities. Information can be passed along by "word of mouth" or within one of a network's regular channels (e.g., newsletters, websites, e-mail blasts, etc.).

Any school, college, church, or membership organization (e.g., American Legion, Rotary Club, Business & Professional Women's Club, etc.) and even the workplace itself can be a network that will keep the job seeker apprised of new and emerging opportunities. These networks often call attention to employment opportunities before they are formally announced.

The federal government, which is the largest single employer in the United States, allows job seekers to search for governmental career positions at the USA Jobs website, which can be accessed at http://www.usajobs.gov/.

Career Fairs

Career or job fairs are events that are sometimes sponsored by institutions, employers, and local or regional government agencies to provide personal contact between job seekers and human resources officials that have or are expecting to have positions available. Many career fairs are held on college campuses in the winter and spring to provide opportunities for upcoming graduates to interface with a variety of potential employers. Often when a new firm moves into a city or community, it will use this type of event to promote the range of employment positions it will have and provide opportunities for applicants to speak with company representatives. Innovations in communication technology are extending the reach of many of these types of programs.

Informational Interviewing

The importance of human information sources in career exploration was addressed previously as a career exploration strategy. Now those and other contacts can be employed as job identification and search sources. Informational interviews should be requested by job seekers to conduct research into an organization and its range of job opportunities. A second-semester junior or first-semester senior student in college might, for example, request an informational interview with a human resources professional to learn about generic positions with the firm and those that may be available at graduation time. Informational interviews, although not focused on a particular vacant position, also allow the interviewer an opportunity to look at the individual as a prospective applicant.

Strategies for Securing Part-Time or Summer Employment

Should you find yourself seeking summer employment or a situation that would allow you to take on a paid position of a few hours a week during the school or college term, there are some strategies that can guide you. Learn these strategies well because it is likely you will be repeating them often over the course of your career.

Take a talent inventory. Do you have a particular ability or skill—like designing websites, working with children, or speaking a second language? Where could you put your special ability to use? Small Internet start-up companies in your area might use your website development talents. Daycare, church, or community programs could have excellent opportunities for childcare assistants. And finally, local libraries, non-profit organizations, consulting companies, and tutoring centers might wish to capitalize on your language skills.

Create and use as many networks as you can. Do you know people who work in companies or businesses that you think might be interesting? Don't be shy: Ask them to check out the prospects of a summer or part-time position for you. Many of the best summer jobs—ones that aren't advertised—are discovered through "people" connections! Just ask around and remember to follow through with phone calls, letters, or e-mails.

Convert knowledge, skills, interests, and talents into job prospects. Cool summer or part-time jobs are often found where you least expect to find them. It's all about making the right connection. Think about companies and organizations where business is likely to increase in the summer months. If you love the outdoors, then state parks and summer camps are a great place to start looking for a summer job. If it's business experience you're after, check with the owner or manager of a firm that interests you and tell them why you'd like to come aboard for the summer. They'll be impressed that you're such a go-getter.

Consider creating your own job. Many summer and part-time jobs are closer than you think. Ever thought about being your own boss? You'd be surprised at how much you can earn by doing things for people. Organize a crew of your friends and create a lawn mowing or babysitting service. Have a flair for cuisine? Plan menus, then prepare, and deliver meal baskets for busy people who don't have time to cook. Think about other "service" ideas that people would pay you to perform for them.

As your own boss, you'll definitely have more responsibilities, but the monetary rewards can far outweigh the extra time and attention you'll devote to these entrepreneurial duties. And beyond the extra dollars, the leadership and management experience you will gain will be priceless.

Student Activity 11.1

Valuable Sources of Job
Information and Networking Opportunities

Create a list of the various sources of job placement information that you may wish to return to one day when you begin your official search. Be sure to include names and contact information of people with whom you have interacted personally, Internet sites, and networking groups.

_____

_____

_____

_____

_____

_____

_____

_____

_____

_____

~

CHAPTER TWELVE

First Steps in the Job-Seeking Process

A good plan is like a road map: It shows the final destination and the best way to get there.

—H. Stanley Hall, writer

Identifying vacancies and employers who are actively seeking people with your talent and skills is just the first part of the process of a job search. Important as that early phase may be, it is the second part of the process that results in successful job placement. This is where the development of job-seeking tools (i.e., résumé, application completion, etc.) and mastery of strategies (i.e., interviewing, networking, etc.) will be required to maximize exposures and enjoy success in personal placement. It involves the job seeker developing a plan of action and embarking on a comprehensive campaign.

Start the job-seeking process with a specific objective in mind. It is far easier to reach a destination if you know where you want to go and can map the alternative ways of getting there. Within the job-seeking plan, make certain you are practicing sound time management strategies, including setting aside a portion of your day or week to conduct research, prepare documents, make calls, and send e-mails. You should also maintain a portfolio of things you create and submit to employers (e.g., résumés, letters, applications, notes, etc.). It also involves the scheduling and participating in and critiquing of interviews. All this should be done before you will hopefully have a range of job offers and make a selection based on your best career interests now and into the future.

Importance of a First-Rate Résumé

An accurate, complete, and reader friendly résumé will often be the job seeker's first means of communicating with prospective employers. Quality résumés open doors, generate interviews, and lead to employment. Weak résumés, however, find their way to the human resources department file drawer or shredding machine. The résumé is the applicant's "face" until he or she appears in person.

While a high school or college student, you should construct a résumé, one that you should always consider "under development" and open to revision as your life, school, and work experiences unfold. As a "living" document, your résumé will grow and change as you engage in new work, education, and life experiences. Never let your résumé rest too long without revision or modification.

Given the short time employers typically take reviewing résumés, you will want to make certain yours contains the "basic" information most are expecting to find there. A typical chronological résumé (information presented in the order of occurrence) will contain the following components or sections:

- Identity and contact information
- Career or job objective
- Achievements and accomplishments
- Education attainment and experiences
- Work experiences
- Talents, interests, affiliations, and activities
- References

The ABCs of Résumé Construction

Employers read dozens—sometimes hundreds—of résumés from applicants. Do everything you can to make yours reader friendly and make it stand out from the rest of the pile. The four basic rules of résumés are:

- Provide enough information to create a true profile of yourself.
- Use the least number of words to describe you and your background. Employers don't have a lot of time to read lengthy résumés. Keep to one or two pages in length.
- Be honest, assertive, and positive without being boastful.

- When appropriate, personalize each résumé you send by changing the objective to reflect what you'd like to do for the employer.

Name: Put your full name at the top of the résumé and provide your full address, telephone number, and e-mail contact information if applicable.

Objective: State your main goal in seeking employment with the firm, organization, institution, or agency you are sending your résumé to.

Education: Identify your highest level of educational attainment or student status. If you have earned a college degree, don't reference high school because it is assumed. If you are currently a student, indicate the expected completion date and anticipated degree, certificate, or diploma.

Employment: List in chronological order (starting with the most recent first), your primary employment experiences to date. Be certain to identify the location (city and state) of your work experiences for an employer to validate your employment.

Related employment and volunteer experiences: List in chronological order any other part-time, summer, or volunteer experiences.

Special talents and skills: List any specific talents or skills you have acquired that might be useful to an employer.

Honors and awards: Identify any special recognition you've received for academic, athletic, extracurricular, or other related activities.

Activities: List two to four things that you do for enjoyment or pleasure. These might be personal (e.g., reading, cooking, etc.) or school, community, or church/synagogue related.

References: If requested, list two to three individuals (i.e., name, company, address, phone, or e-mail) who can speak favorably about you. Obtain their consent before you submit their names to a prospective employer. You want your references to be prepared to give you the best recommendation they can, and no one likes to be caught off guard. Either include the names and contact information of two or three individuals who can speak to your employment or educational experiences or indicate that this information will be provided on request.

Date: Include the date of the résumé creation or revision as a reminder of when you need to update it with current information.

A sample résumé that includes these features follows.

Frank Benjamin
1776 Independence Avenue
Freedom, PA, 17776
717/555-1776 / fbenjamin1776@gmail.com

Objective: To use my skills and interests in graphic communications, desktop publishing, and computers to build and maintain websites and contribute to the information technology needs of a small organization, agency, or business

Education: Freedom High School, member of the class of 2019. Completed four graphic design courses at Jefferson County Community College.

Employment: Green Valley Lawn Service, Freedom, PA—Provided lawn and garden care services to forty-four clients and supervised team of four mowing crew members (summers, 2018/2019), Jefferson County Parks & Recreation Department, Heritage, PA. Served as camp counselor for twenty-five youth campers (summer 2016).

Related employment and volunteer experiences: Sales clerk, Freedom Plaza Walmart (holiday seasons—2007/2019), Unity, PA; Volunteer, Heritage Community Hospital (2018–present), Heritage, PA; Referee, Freedom Community Soccer League (2016–present), Freedom, PA.

Special talents and skills: Created websites, skilled in Microsoft Office, Adobe, and various other desktop publishing programs.

Honors and awards: Freedom High School honor roll (two years), student council representative (junior/senior years), science fair (third place, Environmental Sciences division) 2007.

Activities: Varsity and junior varsity soccer and lacrosse teams (selected by teammates to serve as co-captain during senior year), photography, golf, and fantasy football team manager.

References: Available upon request

04/01/20

Final Thoughts on Résumé Construction and Maintenance

When you believe you have created a quality résumé, put it away for a couple of days and allow it to rest. When that time has passed, put your completed résumé to the following content, style, and readability test. When you are satisfied with the revisions and adjustments you will undoubtedly make, it is ready for distribution to prospective employers.

- How long is the résumé? Most human resources managers would like to see résumés that are not longer than two pages in length. In your quest for brevity, however, make certain not to eliminate any important information.
- How does the résumé look? Is it reader friendly? Have you used a résumé design that breaks up the components and allows for an inviting visual presentation?
- Have you proofread and spellchecked the résumé? Nothing will display your lack of "attention to detail" more than a résumé that contains grammar and spelling errors. Avoid pronoun use (i.e., I, my, me) whenever possible. Have you used complete sentences or fragmented sentences? Either is acceptable, but consistency is required.
- Have you quantified your experiences? Stating that you supervised a team of eight sales representatives is more informative than saying you were merely a supervisor.
- Did you use "action" language, especially verbs, in describing your experiences and accomplishments? Words and expressions like *understand*, *assisted*, and *interested in* are not as convincing as *completed*, *managed*, and *served*.
- Should you consider a functional résumé instead of a chronological one? A functional résumé addresses the knowledge and skills you possess with minimal reference to your experiences. It is often preferred by individuals with gaps in their experience and those reentering the workforce after an absence.
- If responding to a particular position, does your résumé do an effective job of addressing the relationship of your background and experiences to the specific vacancy? For this reason, many résumé creators may need to have multiple versions of their résumé for use in responding to individual opportunities.
- Is your résumé "gap free"? Many individuals have entered, exited, and reentered the workforce for various reasons. Do your best to fill such gaps so as not to generate questions in the mind of the résumé reviewer.
- Have you avoided the trivial and redundant? Playing "Happy the Clown" at the annual summer church bazaar is less important than your

church volunteer and service learning experience. Explain the experience in the briefest possible way. Be sensitive to how many times you say the same thing in your résumé. Once is sufficient.

- Were you honest and forthright as opposed to misleading and boastful? Everything you place in your résumé can be researched and validated. Don't place anything there that isn't accurate and verifiable.
- Have you omitted personal information (e.g., age, sex, ethnicity/race, religion, height, weight, marital status, and health information) or reasons for leaving previous positions? Some of this information is addressed in various federal laws, and employers cannot ask about or use it to screen or select candidates.
- Résumé creators may learn that multiple résumés are in order because using a single profile may not meet the needs of the information requested or needed to get to the interview stage. If this information cannot be added in the cover letter, then a "tailored-to-position" résumé may be best.
- Have you included references? The identification of references typically follows in the job search, and your willingness to provide this information is all that is required on the résumé. Even the inclusion of the "References provided upon request" statement is optional.
- Have you asked a family member or friend to review the résumé? A second set of eyes will identify things your proofreading may have missed. Don't allow any correctible or inconclusive part of your résumé to kill what might otherwise be your best chance of moving along the job acquisition process.

Written Communication as a Job Search Tool

Many believe that letter writing has become a lost art, in some instances replaced by the less formal communication exchanged between parties via e-mail, texting, and other electronic devices. There are at least three types of communication associated with job acquisition that will require the applicant to craft a personal and professional message and deliver it in letter format. They include:

- General letter of inquiry regarding employment
- Letter expressing interest in a particular position
- Follow-up letter to an employment interview
- Formal letter-résumé

Samples of these types of communication (letter and e-mail) follow for your review.

General Letter of Inquiry Regarding Employment
Key features of the letter: Expression of interest in business, firm, agency, or organization. Availability and willingness to interview for relevant positions. Reference to enclosed résumé.

1776 Independence Drive
Freedom, PA, 17776
Date

Ms. Susan Burton, Director of Human Resources
Freedom National Bank
1612 Plymouth Landing
Freedom, PA, 17776

Dear Ms. Burton:

I am writing to express my interest in a position with Freedom National Bank. Currently, I am a second-year student at Independence Community College, enrolled in the degree continuation program. My educational objective is to transfer to Patriot University and study Business Administration.

In particular, I would like to learn of any part-time positions that might be available that would be compatible with my college study schedule and any full-time work I might perform during the summer break. I am particularly interested in the banking and finance field and believe that any experience with Freedom National Bank would contribute to my career pursuits.

I would welcome the opportunity to meet with you to discuss any opportunities and interview for this or related opportunities at Freedom National Bank. My résumé, reflecting work and educational experiences to date, is enclosed for your review. You may contact me at fbenjamin@hotmail.com, 555/765-4321, or at 1776 Independence Avenue, Freedom, PA, 17776.

Sincerely,

Frank Benjamin

Enclosure

Letter Expressing Interest in a Particular Position

Key features of the letter: Expression of interest in a particular position known to be available in the business, firm, agency, or organization. Presentation of educational and work experiences and credentials. Interest in having the opportunity to interview. Reference to enclosed résumé.

1776 Independence Drive
Freedom, PA, 17776
Date

Ms. Susan Burton, Director of Human Resources
Freedom National Bank
1612 Plymouth Landing
Freedom, PA, 17776

Dear Ms. Burton:

I am writing to express my interest in the position of customer services representative with Freedom National Bank. Currently, I am completing my Bachelor of Science Degree in Business Administration at Patriot University and expect to receive my degree this spring.

Over the past two years, I have had numerous part-time work and volunteer opportunities where I have had to work with the public and, in numerous instances, handle money. In addition I have served as Treasurer of the university student government organization and have been responsible for a number of money management tasks and responsibilities. I find this work enjoyable and believe that a banking position and business work environment would be well suited to me.

I would welcome the opportunity to interview for this or related opportunities at Freedom National Bank. My résumé, reflecting work and educational experiences to date, is enclosed for your review. You may contact me at fbenjamin@hotmail.com, 555/765-4321, or at 1776 Independence Avenue, Freedom, PA, 17776

Sincerely,

Frank Benjamin

Enclosure

Follow-Up Letter, Note, or E-mail to Employment Interview

Key features of letter or e-mail: Expression of gratitude for the opportunity to interview. Declaration of continued interest in the position. Offer to provide additional information.

Dear Ms. Burton:

I would like to thank you for the opportunity to interview with the Freedom National Bank for the teller trainee position. The export to the branch office environment and information I acquired from you and your colleagues heighted my interest in work for Freedom National Bank.

Should you require additional information or clarification, please contact me at fbenjamin@hotmail.com or 555/765-4321. I look forward to hearing from you.

Sincerely,

Frank Benjamin

Formal Letter-Résumé

Increasingly, career counselors and staffing professionals are recommending that applicants use a letter-résumé to respond to and apply for specific positions. The basic rules to follow in developing a letter-résumé are:

- Begin your letter in a normal manner by introducing yourself and stating your reason for writing.
- Use bullet points to insert your basic résumé in the body of your letter.
- Close by thanking the addressee and providing information for follow-up.

Completing Employment Applications

There are still quite a few employers that use a standardized application to gather information they wish to collect from job applicants. This will most certainly be the case if you are seeking permanent, summer, or part-time

1776 Independence Drive
Freedom, PA, 17776
Date

Ms. Susan Burton, Director of Human Resources
Freedom National Bank
1612 Plymouth Landing
Freedom, PA, 17776

Dear Ms. Burton:

I am writing to express my interest in a position advertised by Freedom National Bank for a customer service representative and investment advisor. Currently, I am completing my studies at Patriot University and would be available to participate in the Freedom National Bank advisor orientation and training program this coming June.

An overview of my educational and work experiences follows.

- Objective: To use my knowledge and skills in business management and my interests in working directly with consumers in an entry-level professional position in the field of banking, finance, or investment, one that will allow me to progressively grow and develop as an investment advisor.
- Education: Patriot University, Bachelor of Science in Business Administration (2010)
- Relevant work experience: Teller and accounting clerk, University Credit Union (part-time and summers, 2017–2018), Liberty, PA
- Other work and volunteer experiences: Camp counselor, Jefferson County Parks & Recreation (summers 2014–2016), Unity, PA; Sales clerk, Freedom Plaza (Holiday seasons 2007–2008), Freedom, PA; Volunteer, Heritage Community Hospital (2018–present), Heritage, PA; Referee, Freedom Community Soccer League (2016–present).
- Special talents and skills: Microsoft Certified Professional (MCP) certification, website creator, Microsoft Office and related products, various desktop publishing programs.

- Honors and awards: University dean's list (2017–present), re-
cipient of the Patriot Young Business Leader's Scholarship
(2017–2019), Freedom High School honor roll (two years),
student council representative (junior/senior years), Science Fair
(first place, Environmental Sciences division) 2015.

I would welcome the opportunity to interview for this or related opportunities at Freedom National Bank. My résumé, reflecting work
and educational experiences to date, is enclosed for your review. You
may contact me at fbenjamin@hotmail.com, 555/765-4321, or at 1776
Independence Avenue, Freedom, PA, 17776

Sincerely,

Frank Benjamin
Enclosure

employment with national firms such as Walmart, Target, McDonald's, or
Baskin Robbins. Each firm has created an application form that addresses
the information each seeks to have for all applicants. Although the majority
of these applications ask for the same basic information, each is just different enough to require that the applicant stop and complete it. In some
instances, firms will ask applicants to complete an electronic application on
the Internet.

The task of completing a job application is sometimes as simple as trans-
ferring information the applicant has already presented in a résumé and then
addressing any unique questions or requests for information contained on the
application. Be certain to take a copy of your résumé with you at the time of
application because it will allow for the smooth transference of data. Make a
copy of completed applications for inclusion in your career portfolio.

Job Identification and Job-Seeking Skills Are Life Skills

Rare today is the person who starts and ends his or her career in the same
location. Often people elect to move or change either their work or their
employer. In other situations, the circumstances of employment change (e.g.,
layoffs, cutbacks, etc.), and people find themselves seeking other employ-

ment. The ability to practice sound search and identification strategies, as well as talent needed to craft and maintain a quality résumé and the accompanying letters and communiqués, are skills you will use many times as you enter, reenter, or move about the workforce.

Career Myth: Having No Experience Is Detrimental to Entry-Level Job Seekers

It is true that many employers prefer experience in future workers and will stress that factor throughout the hiring process. There are also many, however, who are going to rate your potential for succeeding just as high. This is especially true of employers who have positions involving a preplacement orientation or training experience. This employer is placing greater emphasis on personal characteristics, traits, and potential than on past experience and performance. If you lack work experience, keep an eye out for such opportunities.

Career Fact: Networking Is a Valuable Tool for One to Use throughout the Career Development Process

Networks are connections, your links to information about careers, jobs, and education—just about anything you need to know as you transition through school or college, enter, and progress in your career. Networks are people, and for the most part, the most current and reliable information you can access. Your school, college, church, or synagogue can be a network. All of the groups in which you hold membership are your networks. The greater your participation in these casual and information groups, the greater your chances of using the connections that will have a positive impact on your career.

Frequently Asked Questions

Question: Do human resources and personnel officers really read résumés?

Answer: This is one subject where you will find a lot of conflicting reports. Yes, employers use the résumé to make certain the applicant has the basic qualifications and experiences desired in a particular position. How long they spend reviewing your résumé is another matter. Depending on how many résumés are received for a position, it is probably more accurate to say your résumé will be scanned.

Many use the two- or three-review method of studying résumés. The first review is to determine if basic information is present. If yes, it goes on for a second or third review. When the stack is whittled down to the strongest résumés, those are likely to get a most thorough examination.

Another common strategy is for multiple people to review a large group of résumés and then meet to make comparisons and determine which applicants will be interviewed.

Question: I've heard there are different types of résumés. Which is the best kind for a student to use to obtain part-time or summer employment?

Answer: The résumé presented in this chapter is called a *chronological résumé*, one that lists your life, school, and work experiences in the order in which they occurred. This résumé starts with the most recent experiences and works backward. A functional résumé emphasizes skills that you possess and how those abilities translate to positions you are applying for. A functional résumé is often used when the applicant lacks work experience or has experience gaps in his or her employment history. Students applying for part-time and summer jobs are often required to complete an employer application. Although it may ask for the same information you have built into your résumé, an application must be completed nevertheless. Résumés are useful when you are "cold calling," or contacting firms that haven't posted positions but are places you'd like to work if something were available.

Question: What is the ideal size for a résumé?

Answer: If you were to ask a human resources and personnel manager how long he or she would like your résumé to be, the answer would likely be one page or two pages at the most. The greater the number of career and educational experiences you have had, however, the more difficult it can be to be brief. Just remember that the power of a résumé is in its content and not its length. A comprehensive compilation of your background, qualifications, and experiences, presented in readable format is your primary objective.

Question: How can I use summer and part-time employment most effectively?

Answer: First, you have to begin with the understanding that summer employment or part-time during the school year is usually temporary. Next you must realize that many student-oriented jobs are in the service sectors—like working at the grocery store, waiting tables, or flipping burgers. Occasionally, something dynamic or exciting will emerge, but those types of part-time jobs are the exception rather than the rule.

Most good summer jobs are discovered and obtained during the prior fall and winter months. Use the holiday break and winter period to line up your next summer position or to express interest in returning to the job you held last summer. Conditions of the economy are going to influence summer and part-time jobs and increased competition for those which are available. Act early.

Student Exercise 12.1

Building a Basic Résumé

Use the following template to construct a basic résumé. Refer to the content suggestions presented in the chapter in completing the résumé. Save as a permanent document in your electronic files and update as new information is learned and new experiences are generated. Give consideration to different résumés targeted toward multiple objectives.

Name
Objective
Education
Employment
Related work and volunteer experiences
Special talents and skills
Honors and awards
Activities
References
Date

CHAPTER THIRTEEN

~

Strategies for Successful Career and Job Interviews

A good laugh makes any interview, or any conversation, so much better.

—Barbara Walters, television network
news correspondent and talk show host

The best happens! The employer reviews your résumé or application favorably and invites you to the interview stage. Now you are going to have to put a whole new set of strategies in motion. You are no longer just an applicant; you have moved up the ladder and can now view yourself as a serious candidate for employment.

The manner in which you prepare for and conduct yourself in the employment interview typically ends in one of three ways. You will secure the position, extend your involvement in the hiring process, or eliminate yourself from consideration. The interview affords you the unique opportunity to put the best face on you, the candidate. Yes, the fact that you have moved forward on the job search path changes your status from simple applicant (of whom there were likely many) to candidate (of whom there are fewer).

Preparation for the Interview
Competitive candidates are those who prepare fully for the employment role they are seeking. There are a number of ways to get ready for your formal

interview, and you should employ any and all strategies that will give you an "edge" over your competition. These preparation strategies include:

- Research the employer. Most firms, organizations, agencies, or institutions—the exception being "start-ups"—have a history, reputation, and culture that you should attempt to discover. Examine their website, print information, or anything available that will tell you about their work, vision, and mission. Identify anyone in your "networks" who may be connected internally or externally with the employer and ask them to share everything they know with you.
- Review the published or posted position description again. Understand fully the role the employer has identified and prepare for the interview in a manner that emphasizes your unique qualifications, experiences, and interests. Isolate the experiences that connect you most positively to the role the employer is seeking to fill and any unique characteristics or experiences you possess.
- Determine what questions you will most likely be asked during the interview. Often it is as simple as determining what you would ask if you were the actual interviewer. Make a list of those questions and prepare—at least mentally—your response to each. Also anticipate what you might be asked about your previous experience or capacity to do the work.
- Prepare a list of questions you will want to ask during the interview. Your questions about the employer may, in some instances, be as important as your answers to the interviewer's questions. What you know and want to know indicates how much research you have done and says something to the interviewer about your interest and passion for the position.
- Know where you are going and plan to arrive at least fifteen minutes before the interview. If you must depend on public transportation, give yourself sufficient time to factor things you cannot control. Conduct a "trial run" if you are not familiar with the location. It probably wouldn't hurt to generate a set of directions from www.mapquest.com to guide you.
- Determine how you will dress and present yourself for the interview. Need to get your hair cut or styled? Need to make certain a blouse or shirt is ironed? Do your shoes need polish? Along with selecting the appropriate interview wardrobe, these are tasks that cannot be performed at the last minute.
- Dress in a manner acceptable in the environment you are entering. That may vary from a more casual look for an outdoor or construction

work environment where jeans and work boots would be appropriate to a more formal look for a business setting where you should dress in either conservative business attire (e.g., suit, tie, dress, etc.) or casual business attire (e.g., jacket, open shirt or blouse, slacks, pants, etc.). Refrain from gaudy jewelry and overloading your person with fragrances and perfumes. The interviewer wants to remember you and not your smell. When applying for a professional position, err on the side of being too formal, rather than too casual.

- Good grooming and hygiene are work requirements that candidates must practice, beginning with the interview. Make certain that your hair and nails are presentable and avoid onions, garlic, exotic cheeses, and other detectable ingredients at lunch if you have an afternoon interview.
- Determine if you need to bring anything to the interview. If writing samples, creative pieces, or other items can add to the personal impression you are going to make in the interview, take them with you.

Remember that the hiring decision is predominantly an emotional one. Many qualified and competent candidates will have reached the interview stage along with you. Only one person will be hired or just a handful will be recommended for continued consideration.

Interview Behavior and Demeanor
Employment interviews are conducted for different reasons. In a competitive work environment, employers have to choose among multiple candidates with varying knowledge, skills, and experiences, and their task is to find the most qualified and competent employee, one who will fit into the culture of the organization and contribute productively to its mission.

Some interviews are used to screen candidates, obtain information beyond that which is presented on the résumé or application, and determine if the candidate has the qualifications to warrant additional consideration. Screening interviews can be held either in person or over the phone. In some instances, the screening interview will be conducted by the human resources or personnel department with the strongest candidates "called back" for a formal or structured interview with the supervisor, department head, or the individual to whom the employee will report.

Formal or structured interviews typically have the candidate responding to a series of set questions by the interviewer(s), questions that are intended to examine individual qualifications and experiences to determine the level of fit or suitability for a position. In this type of interview, the candidate's knowledge, skills, and competencies are being compared to expectations the employer has set in seeking to fill the vacant position. Sometimes it will take more than one interview for an employer to determine which candidate is best qualified, and the "call-back" interview typically means a step up in intensity.

There will be situations in which you will be interviewed separately by more than one individual and others when multiple interviewers are present together. Although you will likely know of this structure in advance, don't feel that you are outnumbered or "ganged up on" if multiple individuals represent the employer. It is just the way some organizations approach interviewing.

Some Thoughts about Behavioral Interviewing

Behavioral interviewing occurs when the employer poses hypothetical situations or questions to determine how the candidate responds to real circumstances in the workplace. The response you offer is thought to be indicative of your general thought process and problem-solving ability, processes the interviewer would like to observe and evaluate. Following are several sample behavioral interview questions:

- Describe a time in your work when you were faced with a particularly complex problem. What did you do?
- Identify an experience in your work where you were called on to exert personal leadership to achieve your employer's goal or objective. How did you respond?
- Cite an example of how your personal creativity and ingenuity were called on to address a work-related matter.

When faced with questions that require answers about behaviors you have either used or would use to address a work situation, you should use what human resources managers refer to as the STAR technique, a method of answering an interview question that addresses situation, task, action, and response.

First, think of a situation similar to one in any of the three questions. In stating the situation, you might say, "I recall a situation when our work team was spinning our wheels and floundering, unable to address an important production matter." Next, offer the task or strategy that you offered to remedy the situation. Your response might be that you believed it necessary to go back to the beginning and review what outcomes were desired and what steps would likely result in their achievement.

This would be followed by the action you performed and requested of your coworkers to resolve the situation. Here you might state that you took an active leadership role and organized team members in a way that required each to expend a certain level of energy in developing an effective plan. You might add how you oversaw this effort and the time requirements you set for its completion. Finally, inform the interviewer of the result that occurred from your attention and behavior.

Applying the STAR technique is not difficult but doesn't always play itself out positively in a spontaneous situation. You may have to think of behavior situations in advance, committing the application of the STAR technique in each instance to memory and then interjecting your prepared response into the interview when appropriate.

Anatomy of the Interview
Interviews are typically open-ended, meaning the candidate will not know the questions in advance. Interviewers, however, may identify focal points in advance and encourage the candidate to direct his or her responses toward those issues. Often human resources and personnel managers will provide direction to the candidate by saying something like "Be prepared to address."

There may be some positions (e.g., graphic artist, photographer, etc.) for which the interviewer will ask candidates to present samples or a portfolio of their work at the time of the interview. Finally, some employers may wish to use the candidate's time with them to administer a skills test (e.g., editing, keyboard, etc.) if mastery of certain job functions is essential to employment. You will likely be informed in advance that taking such a test will be required.

There is also an interview etiquette that is worthy of consideration prior to an actual interview. Individuals being interviewed should consider the following personal behaviors, attitudes, and protocols.

- Extend a warm greeting, including a firm handshake, when you meet your interviewer(s), establish good eye contact, and keep a friendly expression throughout. Strong eye contact, positive body language, and an enthusiastic attitude should be maintained at all times. Finally, silence your cell phone or, better yet, leave it in the car.
- Treat the interview as the formal activity that it is, for you and the employer. Being too relaxed or casual can often be misinterpreted as being lackadaisical and disinterested—two surefire ways to kill your chances.
- Be honest, candid, and yourself. You want the employer to hire you and not the character you played during an interview.

- Respond to each question thoroughly and concisely, and use examples to support answers when possible. If you think you have been talking too long, you are probably right. Think in "sound bites" like people do in an appearance before a microphone or camera. Offer a full response using the shortest number of words. Following you will find a number of questions that you might expect to be asked:
  o What are your short- and long-range career goals?
  o Why did you choose this as your career field?
  o What are your personal strengths and attributes?
  o What things challenge you and present the greatest difficulty to you?
  o Do you see yourself as a strong team member or contributor?
  o What motivates you to succeed in your work?
  o In what school and college subjects were you most successful?
  o How are you with managing time and detail?
  o Are you willing to travel?
  o What are the two or three things you want to be present in your work?
  o Describe a highly rewarding experience in your education and work history.

These questions are representative of questions interviewers ask. The list is not intended to be exhaustive. Ask friends and colleagues who have been in the career and job entry process what questions they were asked.

- Interject your questions where appropriate and certainly when asked at the end of the interview. Following you will find a number of questions that candidates often want to know the answers to.
  o What are the current challenges facing the organization?
  o What are the short- and long-range goals of the organization?
  o Why is this position open?
  o What is the organizational structure and to whom would I report?
  o In examining the responsibilities, I would like to know more about _____.
  o How would you describe the ideal candidate for this position?
  o What are the opportunities for growth and advancement?
  o Describe the work environment and corporate culture.
  o What are this organization's greatest strengths?
  o What makes the organization a good place to work?
  o What is your timetable for making a decision and filling this position?

Your preparation research and the interview itself may uncover additional questions that are appropriate. Don't allow the interview to end with them unanswered. Also think about the timing of your questions. For example, don't ask about advancement and promotion before you have addressed your relationship to the position for which you've made an application and established some personal credibility.

- Avoid any discussion of compensation and benefits until it is interjected by the interviewer. In most situations, your research or the employment posting will provide you with a sense of salary range and general benefits in advance of the interview. You may have to answer the question specifically before the interview ends, but it is far better to present your qualifications, experiences, and personality before any money issues are discussed. You may wish to address compensation by stating: "I was hoping to earn a salary in this range, but I'm open to discussion and negotiation about salary." The best scenario would be for you to be offered the position and the compensation to come up as a part of negotiating the terms under which you would accept it.
- Seek clarification when you don't understand a question or need additional direction making your response. Avoid, however, using expressions like "I don't understand the question," or "I'm not sure I know what you mean."
- Avoid being negative. Never speak in derogatory terms about a previous employer or employment situation. Negativism can be translated as whining, and you become a whiner. It is not the image you want to project.
- Generate an image of the coworker or subordinate you may likely be one day. The interviewer is assessing these human characteristics as much as your qualifications and experiences.
- Infuse the information you obtained in your research about the employer. Often this knowledge and the fact that you conducted the research will impress the interviewer.
- Expect respect and courtesy throughout the interview process. Be respectful and courteous in return, expressing appreciation for having reached this place in the hiring process.
- Be sensitive to the fact that federal and state laws prohibit employers from asking some questions. It is illegal to ask questions about such things as age, sex, race/ethnicity, religion, health, marital status, and other matters that are not related to the job. More appropriate would be a more direct question such as, "Are you capable of performing the responsibilities associated with this position?"

- Control your emotions. Searching for a job, as stated previously, can be a time-consuming, frustrating, and, sometimes, stress-generating experience. Being unemployed, in addition, can result in added tension and anxiety. Don't allow emotional factors to enter the interview room with you and affect you negatively. Avoid emotional and mood extremes, and navigate a more central path throughout the interview. Finally, never appear desperate or willing to take any job under any conditions.
- Take notes about important issues or matters, but don't let the note taking distract from devoting attention to the interviewer's questions.
- Allow the interview to help answer the question of whether you would accept employment if offered. You will be amazed how much about an employer you can learn in an hour of direct exposure.
- Enjoy the experience. Remember the Barbara Walters quote at the beginning of this chapter. Should something humorous occur or be said during the interview, don't be afraid to laugh.
- At the close of an interview, make your interest in the position known once again and possibly more firmly than previously. Interviews can affirm for candidates their interest in a particular job and, if that occurs, you may wish to end the interview with a strong affirmation of your interest in the position.

After the Interview: Several Matters that Will Require Attention

The interview has ended. You have shaken hands again, offered your gratitude and commentary on the experience, and departed. In the period immediately following the interview, you should take a moment for personal reflection. What are the things that you did well, and in what areas could you have responded differently or provided a different answer to a particular question? Critiquing your experience, if only a mental review, will prepare you to do a more effective job the next time. Each interview is a learning experience and can teach you some valuable do's and don'ts.

Take the time to write or e-mail a thank you note to the interviewer, expressing once again your enthusiasm and interest in working for the organization. Often a handwritten message on a card can be most effective. If you don't have the best handwriting, a typed or e-mailed message will be fine.

Be certain to provide any follow-up information that may have come up during the interview, such as a list of references that will complete your application and interview, and allow the employer to move forward to the decision stage. Finally, if you have not heard from the employer within the time frame a final decision was to be made, it is appropriate to follow-up by either telephone or e-mail.

Rising above the Competition and Getting Hired

Why do people not get hired? Surveys of human resources and personnel managers consistently report that personality, demeanor, and the individual's self-presentation rank highest in reasons why people do not get hired. Your experience and education, and to some extent your skills, are quantifiable by reviewing your résumé, and the interview will delve deeper into these areas, especially if your résumé was less than forthcoming or complete. But in reality, the interview is your opportunity to put a face on the individual seeking employment. Résumés cannot answer questions. People can! Résumés don't have personalities. People do!

Whatever the reason, the candidate's ability to impress the interviewer(s) will govern his or her ability to compete for the position and eventually get the job. The impression the candidate needs to make is two-pronged. First, the interviewer needs to be convinced that the candidate is capable of doing the work. Of equal importance, however, is the candidate's ability to communicate how well he or she will fit into the culture of the organization.

In this regard, the interviewer is assessing personality and personal attributes in the hopes of determining "fit." When qualified candidates offer that certain "chemistry" and the appearance that they will fit in the existing workplace, they are likely to rise to the top and be hired.

Frequently Asked Questions

Question: Where can I find information about a prospective employer to help me prepare for the job interview?

Answer: One of the best sources of information and one that is absolutely current would be to talk with someone who works there. Ask around your networks (e.g., school, church/synagogue, membership organizations, etc.) and try to identify someone. Most businesses today have a website and many have an "About Us" section or link. Place the name of the business, agency, or firm in an Internet search engine and see what turns up. You might be surprised.

Question: I've heard conflicting information about the discussion of salary in an interview. Some counselors advise not to bring it up. Others say to be prepared to discuss salary if raised by the interview.

Answer: Your investigation of a position and company will likely give you a sense of the salary that is being offered for a particular position. Sometimes you are informed of a compensation range and have to decide if it will meet your salary requirements. The exact salary within that range then becomes a matter of discussion or negotiation once it is determined that you are the person the employer wants to hire.

Raising salary as a discussion point in the interview may be something you will wish to do. Let the flow of the interview dictate your action. Above all, avoid making salary a focal point of the interview. Concentrate on the presentation of your qualifications and experiences and let matters of salary and compensation follow in the hiring process.

Student Exercise 13.1

Interview Prep: A Checklist of Do's and Don'ts

As you prepare for an important career or job interview, complete the following tasks.

NEED TO DO / COMPLETED

_____   _____   Reviewed the position description in detail

_____   _____   Researched employer

_____   _____   Created questions likely to be asked and prepared responses

_____   _____   Created questions you seek to have answered

_____   _____   Identified and prepared items that need to be taken to interview

_____   _____   Prepared notes of important points to be made during interview

_____   _____   Identified interview location and mapped route

_____   _____   Selected interview apparel for interview

_____   _____   Performed needed grooming tasks (haircut, etc.)

_____   _____   Other tasks: _____

Note: Make additional copies of this form for use with each interview.

Student Exercise 13.2

Job Interview Critique

How did the interview go from your perspective? What impression do you think you made with the interviewer? What would you repeat or do differently if given the opportunity to interview again? Use the following rating scale to critique each career interview experience that you have.

Comfort with the atmosphere created by the interviewer
Highly comfortable　　　　　Uncomfortable
5　　　　4　　　　3　　　　2　　　　1

Quality of skills displayed by the interviewer
Highly skilled　　　　　Unskilled
5　　　　4　　　　3　　　　2　　　　1

Satisfaction with the questions asked by interviewer
Highly satisfied　　　　　Dissatisfied
5　　　　4　　　　3　　　　2　　　　1

Satisfaction with the answers you offered to interviewer questions
Highly satisfied　　　　　Dissatisfied
5　　　　4　　　　3　　　　2　　　　1

The level of engagement you felt with the interviewer(s)
Highly engaged　　　　　Not engaged
5　　　　4　　　　3　　　　2　　　　1

Opportunity you were given to provide information about relevant educational or work experiences
Great opportunity　　　　　No opportunity
5　　　　4　　　　3　　　　2　　　　1

Opportunity to ask personal questions and gather additional information
Great opportunity　　　　　No opportunity
5　　　　4　　　　3　　　　2　　　　1

Things you did that you would do exactly the same

_____

_____

Things you would adjust or change in your next interview

_____

_____

Overall impression of the interview
Very favorable   Unfavorable
5   4   3   2   1

Overall impression of employer
Very favorable   Unfavorable
5   4   3   2   1

Response if offered position
Accept enthusiastically   Accept Reject

Comments:

_____

_____

_____

_____

Note: Make additional copies of this form to critique additional interviews.

~

CHAPTER FOURTEEN

Career Growth, Mobility, and Maintenance

Yesterday I was a dog. Today I'm a dog. Tomorrow I'll probably still be a dog. Sigh! There's so little hope for advancement.

—Snoopy, *Peanuts* cartoon character created by Charles M. Schultz

If your career development has progressed positively to this point, there is the strong likelihood that you will have found the position you desire and be progressing through the early stages of a positive work experience. This chapter is more projective and addresses issues that will become important after you complete your schooling, target the career field you wish to enter, and then transition to employment there.

The period that typically transcends through early and mid-adulthood is one of career entry and adjustment. As you progress in your career you will likely assume greater responsibility and be rewarded for both your longevity and length of service (advancement). This period may also see you making personal adjustments in what you do and where you do it (mobility). You may find yourself moving about the organizational lattice and assuming new duties and broader responsibilities (promotion).

Career Movement Has Positive Rewards

Once it was common for an individual to start working for an employer and spend their entire career in the same place. Although that may still happen, contemporary workers are presented with greater opportunities and competition for their services, factors that can contribute to their electing to be mobile. Anywhere you work, the employer makes an investment in you. There are human and dollar costs associated with the hiring and orientation process. Providing mentoring and guidance to you in the early stages of your employment adds to this investment, as do the educational programs and training that is made available to you. Should you decide to move on for any reason, that investment leaves with you, along with the knowledge and competence you possess.

Employers hate to lose valued employees, individuals making a significant contribution to the mission of the organization. In response, many businesses, organizations, institutions, and agencies today have implemented employee retention programs that address a number of the elements that make their organization more "employee friendly." Employee retention efforts look at everything from compensation to benefits to work environment. The goal of these programs, in a majority of instances, is to have a positive impact on the life-work balance of their employees.

You, on the other hand, have a personal responsibility. You have to look out for you and make career decisions that are in the best interests of yourself, your family, and anyone who depends on you.

Growth

In whatever work people do, there is the expectation that factors like loyalty, performance, and experience will lead to career growth and advancement. All workers want to find an employer who appreciates their efforts and acknowledges their contributions to the organization. This can be accomplished through the addition or adjustment of role and responsibilities, often of the type that recognize their contributions. Examples might be moving from junior accountant to senior accountant after a period of time with an accounting firm or from one rank to another within a police department.

When you have chosen your employer wisely and you like the work you do and the environment (culture, colleagues, etc.) in which you do it, you want to see your success open every door of opportunity in that organization. There will likely be times, however, in your career development when you will exhaust all available opportunities within a particular organization, and you must seek external opportunities to achieve your full career potential.

With such advancement, there is often the expectation that one's salary will increase as the individual's value to the organization becomes greater. Rewards, however, need not be limited to salary advances. Often, experience and longevity are rewarded with additional days of vacation leave, employer contributions to retirement programs, and other benefits.

Mobility

Why do people change their career situations? The answers are as different as the people doing the changing. Many move for career opportunity and growth. People also move to find an environment in which they feel comfortable and appreciated. Others may move because they want to consider options that may not be present in their current situation. Consider the following reasons why people move in their careers:

- *Natural movement.* When you have chosen your employer wisely and you like the work you do and the environment (e.g., culture, colleagues, etc.) in which you do it, you want to see your success open every door of opportunity in that organization. There will likely be times, however, in your career development when you will exhaust all available opportunities within a particular organization, and you must seek external opportunities to achieve your full career potential.

  There could be circumstances when you like your work but have a "philosophical disconnect" with the organization. Another situation may find you enjoying the work but not comfortable with the size, structure, or some other aspect of the organization. There could also be a circumstance where people relationships such as supervisor-to-employee or peer-to-peer don't achieve the level of collaboration and cooperation you seek and you don't see them improving any time in the near future. Comfort is a critical part of career success as the happy, satisfied individual is definitely the most productive. Finding one's comfort zone may require movement.

- *The "I-hate-my-job" syndrome.* One day off in the future you could find you are in a career situation that you simply dislike. It may be your first job or the fifth. It may be a job that resulted from poor decision making on your part, one that you didn't research properly before accepting. There will also be circumstances when you like your career but dislike your employment situation. This occurs often as a result of a change in the organizational culture. Suddenly you find the organization is not the one you signed on with at some time in the past.

- *The money lure.* Often reasonably successful and satisfied individuals are lured away from their career situations by the opportunity to earn more with another employer. This occurs in situations where employers are either incapable or unwilling to sustain compensation at competitive levels. Individuals, seeing their peers earning more in other environments, "jump ship" in pursuit of greater monetary rewards.

- *Changing nature of the beast.* People are dynamic, growing, and evolving creatures and it may be that you are not at the place where you need to be and doing the work that you truly want to do. As the career world expands and grows, new opportunities appear on one's personal radar, looking better to the individual than the work he or she is currently doing. People also experience burnout and fatigue in their roles and look for alternatives.

Still other members of the workforce go through what counselors and psychologists have called a "midlife crisis," a period of dissatisfaction with their personal lives and lifestyle. Often this change translates to dissatisfaction in one's career or work and the individual senses a need to escape. To stay mentally healthy, it is probably best that they do so.

- *Voluntary exit or interruption.* Increasingly, workers are experiencing "entry, exit, and reentry" in their career development. This is a common occurrence for women who initiate a full-time career activity following training or education and then "stop out" to have a child and engage in child rearing and family management responsibilities.

  There is growing evidence that greater numbers of men are having similar parenting experiences. Once a level of stability and comfort with the family situation is achieved, these women and men seek to reenter and resume their career or make the adjustments needed for reentry in a different occupational role. The strongest reentry options will be available to those who sustain their knowledge and skills and remain connected to their networks.
- *Forced adjustment.* Economic downturns and recessions hit some businesses, institutions, and organizations in different kinds of ways and affect workers in varied work segments. Studies that examine worker attitudes during these times suggest that they come to a realization that they may have to change careers to get reestablished in the world of work. Often this need to be mobile is forced and unwanted but required when the job market offers nothing but dead-end options.

Any or all of these factors constitute a reason why you might wish to dust off your résumé, activate your networks, and get back into a job search once again.

Maintenance

One's career maintenance is best defined as both keeping current and growing in what you do and the career role that you have assumed. A large part of maintenance is growing the knowledge base needed to be effective in your work. This will occur both formally (e.g., courses, seminars, and other education experiences) and informally (e.g., networking with career peers, reading trade and professional publications, attending conferences).

If people's career role were simply the performance of something they learned and then duplicating it over and over again in a robotic style, maintenance would be nothing more than repetition. People change. Work changes. New ways of doing things emerge, as do the tools and technologies of the workplace. Career maintenance, then, requires the continued acquisition of knowledge and skills far beyond the "basic tools" possessed at career entry. Each workday can influence the next, and the totality of those days can have a positive effect on the individual's personal career development.

Career Moves Are about Lattices and Not Ladders

Before this discussion of growth, mobility, and maintenance is completed, a few more words about career movement are in order. One of the common thoughts about the world of work is that successful individuals "climb the ladder" to success, the image being that you enter near the bottom and climb each rung to a place higher up the ladder. The higher the rung is, the greater the success.

In reality, most career and occupational organizations represent a lattice and not a ladder. Successful people make many horizontal moves as they progress through their career organizations. In fact, experience in multiple positions at one level on the career lattice heightens one's candidacy for promotion and advancement.

Career Fact: Experience Plays a Meaningful Role in a Worker's Career Advancement

Consider the fact that new and entry-level people are to a certain degree "equal" when they enter their respective careers. As they progress in their chosen work, these individuals are going to have a range of career experiences that will distinguish and separate them from their peers. It is these differences, and not the similarities, that make the worker more valuable and attractive to both their present and future employers. In some instances, it is these experiences that will cause one to be promoted. In others, the experience factor will open new and more challenging doors.

Frequently Asked Questions

Question: Is there ever a time when it is too late to change careers?

Answer: People change careers all the time and age should not be a factor. The primary motivation should be that you want to work in a role that is enjoyable and satisfying. In fact, as the life expectancy of Americans continues to get longer, many are electing to stay engaged in their careers, seek a modified way (e.g., schedule, compensation, etc.) of continuing their current career, or elect to try something totally new and different.

Question: How can I ensure that my efforts will result in career advancement and allow me to compete for promotions, raises, and other rewards?

Answer: It starts with doing good work and displaying a work attitude and behavior that tells everyone you are industrious, enthusiastic, and productive. Be an effective team player and a leader of that team if you possess those qualities. Recognition is mostly about visibility—being seen as a productive contributor, one who is committed to the mission of the organization and loyal to the employer.

CHAPTER FIFTEEN

Factors Influencing Career Success

There are no secrets to success. It is the result of preparation, hard work, and learning from failure.

—Colin Powell, US Secretary of State, Chairman of the Joint Chiefs of Staff, and US Army general

The career development process plays out differently for everyone, and success is going to be defined in different ways. For some, success will be achieved when they secure and sustain a career of their liking and achieve the respect of their peers and others. Others will find success in achieving a comfortable or satisfactory position in a work environment they enjoy and contributing to the mission of their employers. Still others will want their career and work to allow them to pursue pursuits outside of work like family, travel, and recreational interests—to name a few.

The Five Factors of Success
Regardless of how an individual defines success, reaching it largely involves the interplay of five factors: knowledge, skill, competence, experience, and satisfaction. Each will play a role in your personal career development and influence the degree to which you achieve your personal potential. Each factor will influence a person's overall career development differently, but in the end, all will be contributing factors to one's individual career success.

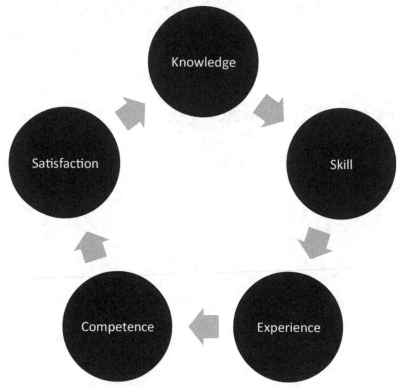

Figure 15.1. The Five Factors of Success

Knowledge

Careers and occupations demand that individuals gain an understanding of the "body of knowledge" that serves as the foundation for their work. Accountants must know accepted business and financial practices; attorneys must know the law; physicians must know medicine; engineers must know physics and other sciences; and so on. Each body of knowledge is unique and different but must be studied and learned if it is to be used in the performance of career tasks. Sometimes there are smaller bodies of knowledge within a larger one (e.g., international law, pediatrics, civil engineering, tax accounting, etc.).

When a command of the body of knowledge is acquired through study, experimentation, and other learning experiences, one is said to possess expertise, both a theoretical and practical understanding of a subject. Knowledge acquisition involves a number of what psychologists call cognitive processes: learning, communication, and reasoning to identify several. Individuals who achieve success in their careers must first acquire and then, maintain knowledge.

Skill

Often used interchangeably or in connection with knowledge, skill takes knowledge to a level of practical application. The attorney who possesses knowledge of the law must also develop the skills needed to practice the law in the defense of clients or as a prosecutor in a courtroom. The same is true for other careers and occupations. Career knowledge and skill go hand in hand. The success of mechanics, mathematicians, surgeons, technicians, and writers is measured in how well they integrate knowledge and skill to produce a harmonious effect.

Some view skill as the practical application or use of knowledge. When people become highly skilled, it is said they perform their career functions expertly and with ease. The skill may vary from writing a computer program to wiring a circuit board to playing a guitar. The common denominator is the mix of knowledge and skill that eventually results in the mastery of tasks in the workplace.

Experience

Experience is measured over time as one performs his or her career tasks and uses the knowledge and skills acquired. It is widely held in many work environments that our career experiences represent a working classroom of sorts where one gets to apply knowledge and skills in practical situations. Experience can also influence how much an individual earns because doing something well consistently can lead to added compensation, promotion, and other forms of recognition.

Competence

The blend of knowledge and skill into successful execution or performance is referred to as *competence*. There are some careers in which competence is measured sequentially with individuals getting better at what they do over time. In other instances, a standard of excellence is needed at the outset. Airline pilots must achieve such a level of competence before they are permitted to assume the "first chair" or fly solo. Often referred to as "zero tolerance for error," many careers demand a high level of competence from the first day on the job.

The higher the level of competence, the greater the accolades and rewards for the individual worker. Monetary compensation is often awarded on the basis of merit, meaning the most productive and highest achievers earn the highest salaries in return for their outstanding efforts.

Satisfaction

A final factor that contributes to career success is the level and extent of satisfaction an individual achieves in his or her chosen career. Satisfaction will be defined and measured differently by every individual. For many, it is doing a quality job and contributing to the success of the firm, institution, agency, or organization that employs them. For others, success is the orderly progression through a series of career stages, each marked by accomplishment and attainment. Finally, for some, it is achieving a place where one's contributions are rewarded in tangible (e.g., salary, benefits, etc.) ways.

Increasingly, US workers appear to be placing a higher premium on the life-work balance. Studies have shown that growing numbers of individuals want to work for employers who promote this equilibrium between the effort and time they devote to their work and that given to their family and the personal aspects of their life.

It must also be recognized that individuals may have to exhibit a degree of mobility and flexibility to achieve maximum satisfaction. Often knowledgeable, skilled, and competent people must move around the world of work to find a setting or environment where they achieve comfort and satisfaction. Career success for them is not achieved until this occurs.

Exercising Power and Control in Achieving Career Success

First as students and then again as members of the workforce, people have the ability to exercise a considerable amount of power and control over their careers. Individuals can pursue any career that matches their abilities, intelligence, aptitudes, and interests. It is about achieving their full educational and career potential. A major part of people's power and control lies in their ability to choose among options and then determine how hard they are going to work at achieving their ambition. The ultimate result can be career success.

Career Myth: Salary Is the Number-One Contributor to Worker Satisfaction

This may have been true in the past, but times are clearly changing. Employers historically rewarded productivity, performance, loyalty, and other characteristics with salary increases, bonuses, and other monetary incentives. Studies show that younger members of the US workforce want their life-work balance needs met and will opt for a flexible schedule or a "quality of life" benefit over increased compensation.

Recent studies by the Society for Human Resource Management (SHRM) and other organizations representing workforce members are pointing to the importance of employee engagement as a key factor in retention. Recognition and respect have moved to the front as matters of importance in building and sustaining employee loyalty.

Don't be misled into believing compensation issues are not important. Every hard-working, loyal employee desires a competitive salary, one consistent with business or industry standards and adjustable over time.

Frequently Asked Question

Question: What are the factors most likely to have an impact on the kind of work that I wish to pursue?

Answer: Any number of economic, cultural, political, and related factors could have a powerful influence on your career and the setting in which you work. It is not unusual for a US work segment to experience periods of growth and decline. The rise, leveling off, and partial decline of the dot.com industry of the 1990s is a perfect example.

Recessions and economic swings (ups and downs) can be extremely influential. A recession, for example, is going to hit certain industries like building and construction, banking, and retail sales much harder than others. A natural disaster such as a hurricane, flood, or tornado could hit unexpectedly and leave chaos and uncertainty in its wake. At the same time, these circumstances and events may also generate opportunities as varying solutions and measures are created to address them. Career explorers, job seekers, and people currently in the workforce need to analyze the potential threat that such events or conditions might pose for them personally and for their work generally and take whatever precautions they can to eliminate or lessen the impact.

CHAPTER SIXTEEN

~

Counselors as Career Development Allies

No matter what accomplishments you make, somebody helps you.

—Althea Gibson, US and international tennis champion (1927–2003)

Professional counselors can play an integral role in facilitating the career development process, and there will be multiple times when that assistance can be used. It is important to recognize what counselors in varying settings do and how each may address a different part of the career exploration and decision-making process and then be available to help individuals enter, succeed, and grow in their chosen career field.

Counselors in Schools, Colleges, and Other Educational Settings

Throughout the schooling experience, counselors function in various ways to facilitate your personal career development. Working in schools, colleges, and related educational settings, these counselors help by:

1. Conducting individual and group counseling sessions that help you:
   - Identify and refine career goals and objectives.
   - Identify personal characteristics and traits that may be relevant to your future career development.
   - Understand the workplace and the many careers that are performed within it.
   - Examine the various educational paths to careers.

- Examine careers that are compatible with the information you are learning about yourself.
- Review findings of standardized tests, interest inventories, and related assessments and their implications for your educational and career objectives.
- Help you relate things you are studying to potential success later in a career.
- Evaluate information, develop educational and career plans, and make tentative decisions.
- Take the steps necessary to implement your educational and career plans.

2. Presenting general information (e.g., publications, videos, and Internet sites) about career and postsecondary opportunities and options or specific information tailored to your personal career goals and objectives.
3. Providing special programs such as career and college fairs, career-shadowing experiences, and exposure to human career resources.
4. Offering transition services aimed at helping you:
   - Apply to schools, colleges, and training programs that will help you achieve your tentative career decisions.
   - Assist you in identifying and acquiring financial assistance in the pursuit of your educational and career goals.
   - Guide you toward part-time and summer employment experiences where you will experience the work world.
   - Apply for employment or graduate school following your initial postsecondary educational or training experience.
   - Help you consider and apply for internships, work, and cooperative education experiences.

Counselors in Community Agencies, Private Practice, and the Workplace

Throughout the time you are studying and again after you have entered the working world, a number of different counselors in community agency, private practice, and workplace settings will be available to offer their professional services in support of the decisions you have made and the transitions you are experiencing.

Counselors working for state and local government typically help unemployed and underemployed individuals with job placement. Many private practice counselors help workers independently assess their career situations, especially circumstances in which they believe they may have chosen poorly or are experiencing personal growth and development changes that necessitate them revisiting all or a portion of the career development tasks they have previously completed. Private practice counselors help their clients deal with a range of workplace adjustment issues (e.g., peer relationships, manager/employee relationships, work-related stress, etc.) that can often be a source of difficulty to one's mental health and impede their productivity at work.

Counselors are becoming increasingly available through the employee assistance programs (EAPs) offered by employers to help individuals deal with adjustment, mobility, work-related issues, people-oriented matters, and other factors that need to be addressed if individuals are to realize their full potential within the organization.

First-Rate Counselors Make a Difference

Quality counselors and counseling services are available to people as they move through the various stages of their personal career development. Counselors can connect explorers and decision makers to information that will result in a better understanding of options and opportunities. They can provide support and assistance during the various transitional periods such as school to college and school to work.

Care should be exercised in using professional counselors by choosing individuals whose preparation is strong and who practice according to the highest-level standards and ethics. Select counselors who hold the appropriate licenses and certification to function in this professional role. Counselors can be an incredible ally throughout the career development process.

Frequently Asked Questions

Question: What types of professional credentials should I look for when selecting a counselor to help me with my career development?

Answer: Professional counselors are those who function according to the professional and ethical standards advanced by the American Counseling Association (ACA) and have been trained in accordance with the standards of the Council for the Accreditation of Counseling and Related Educational Programs (CACREP). They will also possess a professional license issued in the state where they work or a national credential such as the National Certified Counselor (NCC) designation that is awarded by the National Board of Certified Counselors (NBCC). These are the standards that you should look for in seeking counseling assistance.

Question: Why are counselors reluctant to steer me toward a particular educational path or career position?

Answer: Professional counselors are more likely to guide than steer you anywhere. It's your life, your career, and your education, and you need to invest in the strategies that take you into the future. Expect good information and assistance in formulating a career goal and developing a plan to get there, but in the end, expect to assume a major personal role in the exploration, decision making, and transition process.

Question: I am experiencing difficulty separating the things that come to me naturally from the things that I have learned via hard work and personal attention. Will a counselor have tests that can help me with these issues?

Answer: Yes, a professional career counselor will have an array of aptitude and achievement tests, along with a number of interest and values inventories that will provide information to aid you in the exploration and decision-making process. There may also be some personality inventories that will tell you more about yourself so you can determine the appropriateness of considering some occupations and work environments.

Question: Who are lifestyle and career coaches and how can they help me?

Answer: Many professional counselors have adopted what they call "coaching" techniques to use in helping clients move through the career development process. The title *coach*, however, is not one that is defined by most licensure laws, and it has been used by untrained and unregulated individuals to define the work they do and services they perform. To avoid becoming the victim of unprofessional practices by unqualified individuals, check out the counselor's professional credentials and experiences.

Student Exercise 16.1

Tracking Counseling Sessions and Follow-Up Tasks

In the space provided, record notes of your various counseling sessions and any follow-up tasks you must perform.

Date   Notes and Follow-Up Tasks   Completed

_____   _____   _____

_____   _____   _____

_____   _____   _____

_____   _____   _____

_____   _____   _____

_____   _____   _____

_____   _____   _____

_____   _____   _____

_____   _____   _____

CHAPTER SEVENTEEN

~

Parents, People, and the Career Development Process

My mother had a great deal of trouble with me, but I think she enjoyed it.

—Mark Twain, author and humorist

The period of time when students are considering their future and making decisions is filled with excitement, discovery, and sometimes a feeling of being overwhelmed. There is much to be learned and many tasks to be completed. As the various tasks are completed, new ones arise to take their place. Like all of the growth experiences you have had until now, the career development process is one that offers many opportunities for parents and people—some close, some distant at the moment—to play a role.

Parents

Much of the parenting role during the final years of high school and during postsecondary education is typically one of supporting and making certain students are engaged in activities that are consistent with and advance their abilities, aptitudes, interests, and accomplishments.

Let's face it: Your parents want you to do well and achieve all that you are capable of achieving. The agreement, however, may include some contentious or opposing views about the routes you have elected to follow and quite possibly what you have set as your end goal, matters that will require attention and resolution along the way.

Your parents were your first teachers. Then one day they turned those responsibilities over to the formal teachers you now have and the professors who are going to play a vital role in your future. They have not, however, abandoned their educator roles. Parents want their children to learn and practice effective study and time-management skills and make certain you have the tools and resources to do an effective job as a student. It is their role to create an atmosphere that encourages discovery and curiosity and promotes reading, problem solving, experimentation, and expression.

Parents work alongside your teachers and counselors, monitoring your learning experiences and addressing any or all issues that could result in you not achieving your full educational and career potential. They also set the tone for many of the values and preferences you will learn as you experience life at home and in the culture within which you are raised. The "moral" compass you possess is the one most likely handed to you by your parents and your environment.

Although the encouragement, support, and guidance of one's parents is a natural part of the growing experience, you also need the space to grow and learn and become the person you are. There may be points of disagreement and discomfort that need to be addressed. Parents can be particularly difficult to live with when they expect you to be at a particular place in some aspect of your development and believe you are lagging behind.

Keep your parents informed. Let them know the things that interest and excite you and how those things translate into what you want to do in your future work role. When you take action of any sort, keep them informed. This can be anything from selecting courses to study in high school or determining what your "major" field of study will be in college.

Eventually, all must come to the realization that it is your future, and you will be the principal decider about where you go. Students who play a major role in the decisions that affect their future have a greater investment in making those decisions work. It is easier to fail or have mediocre success at the decisions that others make or force on you. The difference between guiding and steering, albeit small, is one parents should recognize and practice. Guiding is an open, promoting, and supporting behavior. Steering is a controlling and dominating one.

Above all, parents and their children must strive for compatible roles and ways of working together throughout the awareness, exploration, and decision-making process. Parents need to be there when needed. Students need to call on their parents for support and guidance. Once decisions are made, however, the student must assume the full responsibility for implementing the decision and bringing it to fruition. In the end, all parties will be proud of the educational and career achievements that have been obtained.

Other Family and Friends

Siblings and other family members, as well as personal and family friends, are often positioned to provide support and guidance similar to that of parents to the individual engaged in educational and career transitions. These individuals represent one of the many networks that have been mentioned throughout this book. Use family and friends as resources when their knowledge or experience is something that has a teaching value.

Educators and Counselors

Life connects each individual with many teachers, professors, counselors, and others who play a formal role in our education, including a handful who will distinguish themselves for the attention they provide and the unique way in which they "connect" with us. These are the men and women who often help you in ways "above and beyond" their routine professional role. These special people in our lives should be included among those whom you turn to for advice and counsel. Theirs is a unique perspective, and their words of candid guidance should be factored into any decision-making formula you are considering.

Mentors and Networks

Throughout one's career, every individual will have the opportunity to interact with and share with many people in the workforce. Mentors are those special people who take a particular interest in our work and in us as a person. The caring, sensitive "hand up" that they offer makes a difference to the new employee coming aboard or to the experienced worker trying to move forward. Over time, these helpers become our networks, serving as valuable sources of knowledge and skill sharing. They should be cultivated throughout your school, college, and work experiences.

Mentors can range from experienced teachers in schools and colleges to veteran managers and supervisors in the workplace. They are living, breathing role models—doing what you aspire to do. Often they are your older, experienced colleagues, individuals willing to take you "under their wing" in the early stages of your entry into a new career or career role.

Regular, Ordinary, Everyday People

From adolescence through the remainder of your life, you are likely to interact regularly with people who will influence you and your work. Some you will meet just one time, and others more frequently. Often these will be formal connections, but they are just as likely to be casual. Take every opportunity to learn from these people, ask questions, and consume whatever wisdom they will share with you about their life experiences.

Your parents, family, friends, and every person you meet in your life experience possess the potential to be a teacher or mentor or to play a similar role in your career development. They will have both formal and informal roles and relationships with you. When you are around them, soak up as much educational and career knowledge as they are willing to share. You will never regret the couple of minutes you took to ask a question or listen to their answer.

As much is to be gained from the people in your life, especially those who serve as your mentors, remember that one day you must return the favor. Share with others just as you have been the beneficiary of those sharing with you.

Frequently Asked Question

Question: There is a history of members of my family working in a particular career field, and I sense a pressure to follow them. Unfortunately, the occupation my parents would like to see me pursue doesn't interest me in the slightest. How do I deal with this?

Answer: Previously in history, work was sometimes viewed from the perspective of a family tradition. Sons followed fathers into the workplace and then raised their sons to follow them. Today, children could feel certain pressures to follow their parents to their alma mater and then into their career field, possibly even into a family business if such an enterprise were to exist.

If there was ever a time to make a case for one's individuality, this is it. Help your parents to learn about—and hopefully grow to appreciate—your unique personal traits, interests, and other characteristics. Parents, for the most part, will want you to achieve your full educational and career potential in an endeavor of your choosing. It is, however, your life and career. Often family conflict of this nature is tied to not what you have elected to study or the career you wish to pursue but rather the reality of your goal and extent of your ambition. A fully considered and planned career goal is more defendable than something less so.

CHAPTER EIGHTEEN

~

Some Closing
Thoughts about Expectations

Luck is a matter of preparation meeting opportunity.

—Oprah Winfrey, entertainer and entrepreneur

You probably know someone who has expressed early on, in bold and un-wavering terms, what they wanted to study and eventually do in their career. You, in fact, could be that person yourself. Similarly, you or others may appear clueless at this point in your life about the future. Those differences are not uncommon and reflect the change and maturity that plays a part in this process.

For those committed to a career, keep testing your interest and the quali-ties of the work that have drawn you to it. Those tests will either strengthen your resolve or tell you to begin broadening your view in search of something else. Adolescents and young adults, unclear about their career futures, should use this time in their lives to gain a sense of self-awareness, expand their knowledge of opportunities and options, and point themselves in the direc-tion of sound goals and objectives.

What role do chance and luck play in career development? Think of them as opportunity, something unexpected that happens to cross your career path. Opportunity to one may not appear as opportunity to another. Two individuals could be exposed to the same life or educational circumstance and take different meaning away from it. One person's junk, it has been said, is another person's treasure.

Exposure to opportunity is another matter, one that should never be considered lightly or dismissed. The more life "intersections" you pass through, the greater the number of opportunities and options you may experience. That is why networks have been identified throughout this book as mechanisms for learning about and taking advantage of career opportunities. Make it part of your life experience to place yourself in the learning, social, cultural, and other intersections that will influence your career positively.

Navigating Your Personal Life Experience

There are some things that you can expect to experience as you navigate yourself to a career and find success and satisfaction in that work. The more knowledgeable you are about their presence and the role they play in your personal career development, the more likely it is that your personal development will proceed smoothly and without altercation.

If your career development proceeds along a normal course, expect to:

1. Devote considerable time to the awareness, exploration, and decision-making tasks before your career future becomes clear and focused.
2. Experiment and expose yourself to any number of real work, volunteer work, service learning, and other situations that offer you the hands-on information that is often your strongest teacher.
3. Expect to be confused and perplexed by the seemingly large number of options that appear positive at first glance and worthy of additional consideration. Each option may require a level of examination before it is advanced as a possibility or dismissed as not realistic or feasible. Allow time on your career development calendar to give full consideration to these options, or someday in the future you may wish you had.
4. Study, study, and study even more. Your immediate career success and security and that which is extended long into the future will be increasingly dependent on the emergence of new knowledge and skills and your abilities to keep abreast of a changing, dynamic set of circumstances that will impact your individual career as well as the entire US workplace.
5. Store learning away to be used one day in the future. Often we study things that appear useless and irrelevant at the time, only to reach into our mental file cabinet at some point in the future and retrieve them. All of a sudden, something that you thought to be "trivial" is helping you make a decision or take a career action.

6. Seek and use the information about education and work that comes in varied formats and a rich mix of sources. Further, expect to accept the help offered by counselors and educators as you transition through each of the stages of your life and career.

7. Experience frustration, disappointment, and possibly even failure along your career path, but approach anything negative with a problem-solving mentality, one that will allow you to get up, dust yourself off, and move on with your personal career development. Do everything you can to identify remedies for any of the issues and problems you might encounter and seek the assistance of professional counselors trained and experienced in guiding people toward effective solutions.

8. Accept the support and guidance of your parents, family, friends, coworkers, counselors, educators, and others as you move forward in pursuit of your goals. Allow them to contribute where appropriate, and don't forget to thank each for their contribution to any measure of success you might achieve.

9. Expect the world in which you live and work to change dramatically between now and the time you achieve what you determine to be your personal career goal. You will enjoy many of those changes and be challenged by others. Ride change like a roller coaster, experiencing every up and down, and feel refreshed and invigorated at the end of the experience.

10. Maintain life-work balance. Your career will be a major life activity, one that will influence family, home, friends, and other factors beyond just you. Throughout your career and life, make certain that your needs are being met and your priorities remain in focus. It is a personal, emotional, and social balance that you will appreciate the longer you experience it.

Hopefully the *Bound-for-Career Guidebook*, with its information and exercises, points you in the direction of opportunities and options that are realistic, desirable, and achievable. The career development process is like a long and winding road, and you have many miles ahead of you. May your travels be enjoyable, and may you achieve every bit of your educational and career potential.

~

Appendix

Career and College Websites

The Internet can provide valuable information and assistance to students engaged in the career and education transitions.

Unfortunately, web addresses are constantly evolving and some on this list may have become inactive or adopted a different Web address. Every effort has been made to create a list of accurate and active URLs at the time of publication. Also note that many websites require users to register before using services or accessing information. For privacy reasons, readers may elect not to visit these sites.

Career
Career exploration, www.careeronestop.org
Job boards/job search
www.careerbuilder.com
www.careerweb.com
www.greenjobengine.com
www.helpwanted.com
www.indeed.com
www.jobpile.com
www.jobweb.com
www.justjobs.com
www.linkup.com
www.monster.com
www.mosthired.com

www.myperfectresume.com
www.recruiting.jobvite.com
www.simplyhired.com
www.usajobs.gov
Military careers, www.todaysmilitary.com
Occupational Outlook Handbook, www.bls.gov/ooh
Occupational Outlook Quarterly, www.bls.gov/opub/ooq/ooqhome.htm
Women's career issues, www.dol.gov/wb/

College

Accredited institutions, www.ope.ed.gov/accreditation
Admission testing and testing alternatives
    ACT, www.act.org
    College Board, www.collegeboard.com
    Fairtest (List of test optional institutions), www.fairtest.org/optinit.htm
    GED Testing Service, www.acenet.edu/AM/Template.cfn?Section
      =GED_TS
    Test Prep, www.number2.com/exams/sat/index.cfm
Common Application, www.commonapplication.org
College exploration/search
    www.asa.org.plan
    www.collegeview.com
    www.college-scholarships.com
    www.howtogetin.com
    www.nces.ed.gov/collegenavigator/
    www.pathwaystocollege.net
Higher education lists
    www.schoolsintheusa.com
    www.yahoo.com/Education/Higher_Education/Colleges_and_Univer
    sities
Catholic colleges, www.catholiccollegesonline.org
Historically Black colleges and universities, www.wikipedia.org/wiki/
    List_of_historically_black_colleges_and_universities
Hispanic serving institutions, www.hacu.net/assnfe/CompanyDirectory.
    asp?STYLE=2&COMPANY_TYPE=1,5
Community colleges, www.en.wikipedia.org/wiki/List_of_community_
    colleges
Christian colleges, www.collegestats.org/colleges/christian
Women's colleges, en.wikipedia.org/wiki/Women%27s_colleges_in_the_
    United_States

National Association for College Admission Counseling, www.nacacnet.
org/studentinfo/Pages/Default.aspx

Financial Aid

General scholarship and financial aid
www.college.gov
www.finaid.org
www.fastweb.monster.com
www.college-scholarships.com
www.students.gov/STUGOVWebApp/Public
www.fafsa.ed.gov
www.wiredscholar.com
International scholarships, www.InternationalScholarships.com
Scholarship Scams, www.ftc.gov/scholarshipscams

Student Issues and Needs

Minority students
African American, www.uncf.org and www.thurgoodmarshallfund.net
Hispanic, www.hacu.net and www.hsf.net
Native American, www.aihec.org
Students with disabilities, www.heath.gw.edu andwww.ncld.org/parents-
child-disabilities
Study skills, www.how-to-study.com/

General

Census Bureau, www.census.gov
Federal Consumer Information Center, www.publications.usa.gov
US Department of Education, www.ed.gov
US Department of Labor, www.dol.gov

Job Boards and Job Search Engines

The following job boards, culled from articles and stories that attest to their
utility, are among the Internet vehicles that help individuals explore job
vacancies and make applications for employment. Where applicable, the occupational or user focus of the site is included in parenthesis.

CareerBuilder.com
CollegeRecruiter.com (current college students and recent graduates)
CoolWorks.com (environmental jobs)
Craigslist.com

Dice.com (technology jobs)
energyjobline.com (energy jobs)
ihireEngineering.com (engineering jobs)
Flex.Jobs.com (freelance and special arrangements)
Goodfoodjobs.com (hospitality and food service)
Idealist.com (internships and volunteer positions)
Indeed.com
Internships.com (internships)
Jobs.google.com
Linkedin.com
Linkup.com
Mediabistro.com (communications and media)
Monster.com
OneWire.com (finance, account, and technology careers)
https://jobs.prsa.org (communications, media, and public relations)
SimplyHired.com
TalentZoo.com
Upwork.com (independent contractors)
USAjobs.gov (federal government jobs)

Career Ability, Interest, and Personality Inventories
Any number of career assessment tools may be used by professional counselors helping clients to explore career and education opportunities. The following list is not representative of the breadth of those instruments but does identify a number of free assessments that can be self-administered.

Career Maturity Inventory, www.vocopher.com

CareerOneStop, www.careeronestop.org/ExploreCareers/SelfAssessments/FindAssessments.aspx

O*NET Ability Profiler, www.onetcenter.org/AP.html

O*NET Skills Profiler, www.careerinfonet.org/skills/default.aspx?nodeid=20

O*NET Interest Profiler, www.onetcenter.org/IP.html

O*NET Work Importance Locator, www.onetcenter.org/WIL.html

Keirsey Temperament Sorter, http://www.keirsey.com/aboutkts2.aspx

Career and College Guides and Directories
Following is a list of popular career and college publications with the names of the publisher in parenthesis following each title. One or more of these titles will likely be found in public and school libraries. The guides and di-